NAVEL GAZING

HOW REVEALED BELLYBUTTONS OF THE 1960S SIGNALED THE END OF MOVIE CLICHÉS INVOLVING NEGLIGEES, MEN'S HATS, AND FRESHWATER SWIM SCENES

BY KIM R. HOLSTON

BearManor Media

Albany, Georgia

Navel Gazing: How Revealed Bellybuttons of the 1960s Signaled the End of Movie Clichés Involving Negligees, Men's Hats, and Freshwater Swim Scenes

Copyright © 2015 Kim R. Holston. All Rights Reserved.

No part of this book may be reproduced in any form or by any means, electronic, mechanical, digital, photocopying or recording, except for the inclusion in a review, without permission in writing from the publisher.

Published in the USA by
BearManor Media
P.O. Box 71426
Albany, GA 31708
www.BearManorMedia.com

ISBN: 1-59393-563-3

Printed in the United States of America

NAVEL GAZING

HOW REVEALED BELLYBUTTONS OF THE 1960S SIGNALED THE END OF MOVIE CLICHÉS INVOLVING NEGLIGEES, MEN'S HATS, AND FRESHWATER SWIM SCENES

TABLE OF CONTENTS

Acknowledgements	xi
Foreword by Jessie Lilley	xiii
Prologue	xvii
Chapter 1 Navel Art	1
Chapter 2 Nighttime Nymphs: The Golden Age of Negligees	77
Chapter 3 Hats Off!	97
Chapter 4 Swimmers	117
Epilogue	127
Appendixes	
A: Freshwater Swim Scenes Quiz	135
B: Gallery of Stills	137
Endnotes	175
References	191

IN MEMORIAM

Ingrid Pitt
1937–2010

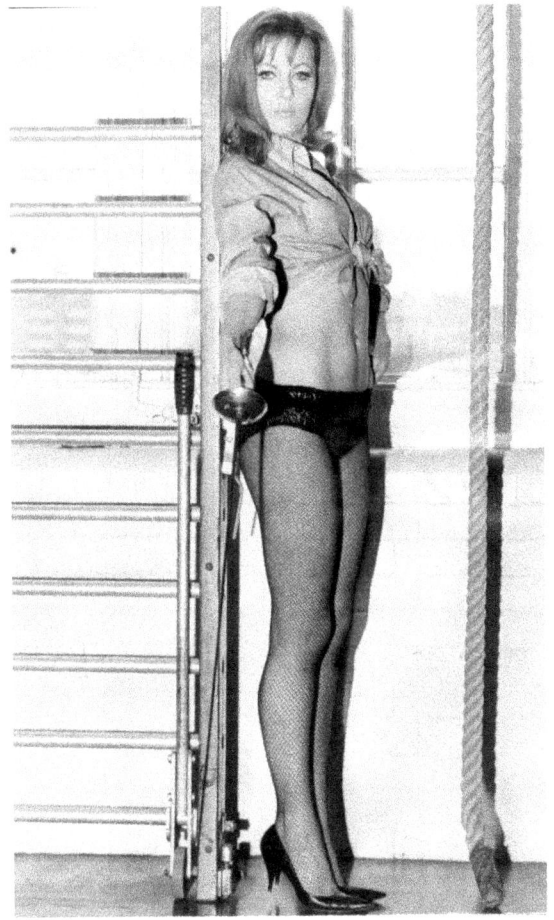

Ingrid Pitt publicity shot, *Where Eagles Dare* (MGM, 1969)

ACKNOWLEDGMENTS

My thanks to Sally (Forrest) Frank, Gail Gerber, Coleen Gray, Anne Helm, Anne Randall Stewart, and Bradford Dillman for fascinating tales of filmmaking in the 1950s, 1960s, and early 1970s. Thanks for the encouragement of teachers and movie mavens Stephen Miller and Keith Smith,* teacher and poet Warren Hope, noir aficionado Tom Winchester, and Michell Muldoon. And, as always, my gratitude to my wife, Nancy—an invaluable sounding board and consultant.

FOREWORD
BY JESSIE LILLEY

I've read through this book a few times now, and find that as usual, politics will cause an argument. That having been said, let me also state that I agree with Kim's underlying thesis, but trouble-maker that I am, I will expand on his basic points.

Let's be factually accurate and change one of his sentences to ". . . mendacious politicians using fear of Communists (read extraterrestrial aliens in many films) and Nazis [often mad scientists] who survived the war…"

Real life Jewish politicians were worrying about Communists, but they were also worrying about Operation Paperclip that was bringing lots of Third Reich scientists over to the USA. It's no surprise that Jewish producers might worry about Nazi mad scientists as much as the red hordes in these films. Leave us not forget that gem, RED PLANET MARS which has the Nazi mad scientist working for the Commies! And what about the racist images in 1950s Sci-Fi? Do not the monster and alien make-ups remind us of the slant-eyed devils we'd just atom bombed in Japan?

Finally, to be completely politically incorrect, leave us not forgot to mention the war of the sexes that was an overwhelming force in the genre back then. To quote Brad Linaweaver, "But why look for feminist subtext in a movie that Joe McCarthy might like?"

I digress.

It's true, times were changing and movies had to follow suit.

The phenomenon of the disappearing naval is one that has been discussed many a time, no question. But rarely with such enjoyable recollections from the women who helped to rediscover this basic part of human anatomy. The rediscovery began in 1959, according to our host, and soon it once again burst forth upon the film-going public, bedecked in jewels, peeking out coyly from just above a bathing suit's bottom… the list goes on and on.

The following pages are filled with lighthearted remembrances from some of the pretty and talented actresses that filled the silver screen in the 50s, 60s and 70s (and some are still doing it). Stories like belly-button rubies breaking loose and escaping to the safety that can only be found under costumers' sewing machines, are laugh out loud funny.

The art work is chosen with love and care, the photos magnificent in their confirmation of the prose—all in all, this is a fun read; a light-hearted diversion from the every day.

So, having dispensed with the politics (briefly), it's now time to join the fun. Ingrid Pitt would have loved this book.

—*Jessie Lilley*

PROLOGUE

It is well known that the 1960s was a decade of social upheaval in the United States. The Vietnam war, racial injustice, inequality for women—those issues boiled to the surface and transformed the country. No less changed in the 1960s was the U.S. motion picture industry. Society affected and was affected by the movies. "Hollywood" had gone through a storm in the 1950s, trying to survive and prosper after the Supreme Court of the United States ruled in the 1948 "Paramount Decree" that, among other rulings, studios must stop forcing unwanted films on exhibitors. Equally distressing for the film industry was the increasing number of ways the public could be entertained. Television became available to the public via the CBS and ABC networks in 1948, and it progressively kept more and more people at home.

Hollywood in the fifties countered competition with on-location filming—much of it in color. The studios employed ads of often sublime ballyhoo. For instance, 1953's *Invaders from Mars*: "From Out of Space…came hordes of green monsters! Capturing at will the humans they need for their own sinister purposes! A General of the Army turned into a **Saboteur!** Parents turned into…rabid **Killers!** Trusted police become…**Arsonists!** Told in a panorama of fantastic, terrifying **COLOR!** " Or 1956's *World Without End*: "CinemaScope's FIRST SCIENCE-FICTION THRILLER! ZOOM across a black sky…quicker than light…faster than time…until you catch up with THE YEAR 2508 on a nightmare Earth of the fabulous future!" This era of transition can be discerned in the fact that no one had, as yet, settled on the term *mutants*. In *Invaders from Mars* it was Helena Carter's Dr. Pat Blake crying, "Mootants! What would they want here?" In *World Without End* it was Nelson Leigh's Dr. Galbraithe: "We took refuge in your tunnel because we were attacked by savages. Mu-tates, we took them to be." Of course, there's the subtext of alarm and paranoia caused by politicians. The mendacious ones used fear of Communists (read extraterrestrial aliens in many films) as well as the uneasy admiration of the science that not only helped win the war but also spawned weapons of mass destruction for instant annihilation or slower death via radioactivity.

Concurrently, technology arrived in the forms of Cinerama, CinemaScope, VistaVision, Todd-AO, and a host of other big-screen processes to lure people back into the theaters. But nothing retrieved the audiences of the mid-'40s, when 90 million people a week attended the picture shows. Emasculated, the major studios crept into the 1960s, finally using Cinerama for films with plots (*How the West Was Won*, *The Wonderful World of the Brothers Grimm*) and making gigantic reserved-seat "roadshow" extravaganzas, many of which actually succeeded, e.g., *Spartacus*, *West Side Story*, *Lawrence of Arabia*, *The Sound of Music*, *Oliver!* But, as the decade rolled along, bigness meant less and less. Baby boomers were dissatisfied; they knew or sensed that European, Japanese, and Indian films provided a more realistic examination of life. Hollywood films remained compromised by censorship essentially unchanged since the Motion Picture Production Code took effect in 1934. It had been challenged, of course, notably via double entendres and Jane Russell's cleavage in Howard Hughes's *The Outlaw* (1943), risqué costumes (but not navels) in *The French Line* (1954), and by the use of the words "virgin" in *The Moon is Blue* (1953) and "panties" in *Anatomy of a Murder* (1959). Times were changing, and movies had to follow suit.

Continental films with the likes of Gina Lollobrigida and Brigitte Bardot were making small but significant waves in the United States. And the British were churning out the gritty "kitchen sink" films of supposedly real life in such items as 1959's *Look Back in Anger* and 1962's *A Kind of Loving*. Pithy political and cultural satires, superbly cast with the likes of Ian Carmichael, Peter Sellers, Terry-Thomas, and Alastair Sim, were also on tap. See *I'm All Right, Jack!* (1959), *School for Scoundrels* (1960) and *Only Two Can Play* (1962).

By the mid-1960s Hollywood was primed to break the

censorship shackles. In 1966's *Who's Afraid of Virginia Woolf?* a blocked portion of the ad read, "Important Exception: No One Under 18 Will Be Admitted Unless Accompanied By His Parent." (Note the "His"!) For this and some forthcoming films, the Motion Picture Association of America (MPAA) devised the SMA (Suggested for Mature Audiences) rating. The following year was a watershed. The sexual element of *The Graduate* and the violence of *Bonnie and Clyde*, both immensely successful films critically and financially, were straws breaking the camel's back. Some Production Code folks saw the writing on the wall. The youth market would be necessary for Hollywood's survival. In 1968, the MPAA replaced the Code with a comprehensive new rating system, which included R for excessive violence, cursing, and nudity.

In this volatile and seemingly more adult and realistic environment, various movies, in retrospect, seem positively antediluvian. See, for instance, *Madison Avenue*, a 1962 black-and-white film that was no more than a "programmer" despite the powerhouse cast of Dana Andrews, Jeanne Crain, and Eleanor Parker. The decline of the classical Hollywood studio system had left those three certifiable stars somewhat in the lurch. Certainly Crain, the former Miss Long Beach and cutie pie of *Home in Indiana* (1944), *Margie* (1946), and *Apartment for Peggy* (1948) had become a voluptuous, and, to use a fifties descriptor, *stacked* woman. Crain was also a proof of an axiom that the nose makes the woman. (For other examples of nasal excellence, see Ingrid Bergman, Susan Hayward, Ingrid Pitt, and today, Scarlett Johansson.)

In any event, Crain's attire in *Madison Avenue* is symbolic. Consider her cosmetic, hardly utilitarian hair netting, the white gloves, and the pearls. Ah, the pearls. Costar Parker wore virtually the same strands. It might be premature to say that Andrews is often hatless and therefore a portent of a coming phenomenon. Obviously he'd checked his fedora before entering the dining room at this Filibuster Bar, where he and his chums imbibe and puff away. Nevertheless, in the rest of the film, Andrews mostly goes hatless but sometimes holds his chapeau. Crain keeps popping up, with and without the pearls, usually in a hat, varying her white with black gloves. But this age of little black and white movies and hats in cinema and society is almost over.*

Jeanne Crain, Dana Andrews, *Madison Avenue*
(20th Century-Fox, 1962)

Other, bigger budgeted dramas, especially those that had been known as "women's pictures" and "tearjerkers," were also on the way out. The *Back Street* remake of 1961, for instance, could hardly have been imagined being made a decade later. Ditto the same year's *By Love Possessed* and 1965's *Love Has Many Faces*, both with Lana Turner. Nor could the 1964 Harold Robbins-based "soaps" like *Where Love Has Gone* or *The Carpetbaggers* that turned turn up in the 1970s. To be accurate, however, Robbins' *The Love Machine* did appear in 1971, but without any big stir or grosses. *Valley of the Dolls* (1967) was, of course, a high-altitude and financially successful soap opera based on Jacqueline Susann's steamy bestseller, but the suggested cinematic titillation was only present via Sharon Tate exercising to keep her breasts firm and Patty Duke doing drugs. Tate didn't really bare a breast, and Duke's half-slip covered her navel. On the other hand, there's something to be said for the symbolic nature of the cat-fight between Duke's young Turk (in real and reel life) and Susan Hayward's aging star (in real and reel life). Duke's ripping off of Hayward's wig marks the end of the era of such characters and films, increasingly viewed as out of touch and dull despite the subject matter.

Even the sprightly, highly amusing, often trenchant, and filmed-in-color comedies of Doris Day and Rock Hudson—*Pillow Talk*, *Lover Come Back* and *Send Me No Flowers*—can in no way be imaged being made after the mid-1960s. Similarly valid then but not later were such other comedies as *Come September*, *All in a Night's Work*, *Ask Any Girl*, *Who's Got the Action*, *A New Kind of Love*, *Love is a Ball*, *If a Man Answers*, *Honeymoon Hotel*, and *That Funny Feeling*.

The same was true of genuine B—low-budget—movies that were still made in the early and mid-sixties, including such small-scale, set-bound westerns with veteran stars from producer A. C. Lyles as *Black Spurs*, *Town Tamer*, *Johnny Reno*, *Waco*, *Hostile Guns*, and *Buckskin*. They served a purpose. For instance, the manager of West Chester, Pennsylvania's Harrison Theatre, said he liked to book westerns because they appealed to the Puerto Rican employees of the local mushroom farms. Nevertheless, such low-budgeters would disappear from the big screen by the decade's end. By the close of the ensuing decade, space opera and fantasy would substitute for riding the range.

What is more germane to this evaluation, a number of movie clichés and conventions could no longer hold. Like certain films, they too seemed silly, shopworn, out of time, naïve. Women in negligees? Men in hats? Rustic swim scenes? Bejeweled bellybuttons? Other than in period films, and sometimes not even then, these time-honored formulas disappeared from the screen at the same time.

Not generally inclined to hidden messages because there may be none—or none of any interest—I have nonetheless posed subtextual meanings when deemed appropriate or possible. Nevertheless, while this tome is full of facts and movie lore, it is designed to be as much fun as educational. Enjoy!

CHAPTER 1
NAVEL ART

"And sailing towards her India, in that way
Shall at her fair Atlantic navel stay;"
—John Donne, *Elegy XVIII: Love's Progress*

THE TWENTY-FIRST CENTURY GOES EASY ON BELLYBUTTONS. They are ubiquitous, and not only with those wearing bikinis. There are joggers and beach volleyball-playing Olympians, bikinied celebrities on magazines and websites, and reality TV contestants. Exercise DVDs feature belly dancers and physical fitness mavens. It wasn't always this way, especially on U.S. movie screens, when for almost three decades the female navel did not exist.

PRE-CODE, AKA PRE-NAVEL HOLLYWOOD

When the movies were young, they were quite liberal—some would say daring. Nudity was not especially uncommon before 1934. For instance, in 1921's *The Four Horsemen of the Apocalypse*, Rudolf Valentino's Julio paints bare-breasted young women in his studio on the Marne. In the 1925 version of *Ben-Hur*, topless—and navel-revealing—young women distributing flowers precede Judah and Arrius in a triumphal parade.

In *Trader Horn*, 1931's seminal Dark Continent adventure actually filmed in Africa, the explorers encounter bare-breasted native women. As for Nina (Edwina Booth), the "white goddess" of the Isorgi tribe, she was practically topless, with an odd, not-very-attractive clump of feathers or animal hair barely covering her chest. Her back was also

Duncan Renaldo, Edwina Booth, Harry Carey, Mutia Omoolu, *Trader Horn* (MGM, 1931)

bare and, one might say, perhaps there's a navel peeking over her furry skirt.

Like darkest Africa, the exotic isles of Polynesia gave filmmakers latitude for risqué expression. More than peeking over her grass skirt was the navel of Dolores Del Rio in *Bird of Paradise* (1932). Mexican born, therefore somewhat of an exotic to gringos, Del Rio was a major star—perhaps the most famous Hollywood leading lady to reveal her navel on screen in the Pre-Code era, and possibly the only one to do so for the following three decades. (The traditional sarong worn by Dorothy Lamour in *The Hurricane* and her "Road" movies with Bing Crosby and Bob Hope gave no scope for bare midriffs. The quasi-sarongs of Maria Montez in her exotic escapades, while they sometimes revealed the belly, did not dip below the navel.) In *Bird* Dolores played the sparkling Luana, Polynesian princess who bewitches visiting sailor Johnny (Joel McCrea) in one of his many classic films.[1] Johnny was overwhelmed by the alluring Luana: "*I thought I just had a yen for ya. I thought this is only gonna be a lark. Oh, but I love you, Luana. I love you more than I've ever loved anyone, more than I ever could love anyone.*" His initial meeting with this enchantress occurs during a nighttime feast when the sailors and leering native men are entertained by wild hootchie-koochie dancing, at the conclusion of which the Polynesian bucks scarf up the mock-protesting women and carry them into the palms. Later, enjoying a cigarette on his ship, Johnny observes a nude female shape swimming under the water. It's Luana and he joins her.

During the earlier dancing, Del Rio wears a sarong, but later, performing before the tribe and its elders, she reveals her navel above her grass skirt. Her back is bare, her bosom covered only by two leis. When she absconds with McCrea to the idyllic island of Lani, she romps in this attire for quite some time. The two-page September 8, 1932, *Boxoffice* ad featured an illustration of Del Rio in this getup, held by a muscled McCrea who apparently is fully nude. A margin illustration depicts bare-breasted wahinis. Announced the ad:

> A NEW RECORDMAKER!...
> Yes, even the "Bring 'Em Back Alive" records...the year's *high spot for every house*...give way to "The Bird's" triumphal sweep across America!

Dolores Del Rio, *Bird of Paradise* (RKO, 1932)

Until the mid-1930s, darkest Africa or its backlot simulacrum continued to permit filmmakers to include outright nudity. In *Tarzan and His Mate* (1934), Maureen O'Sullivan's Jane wore a rather skimpy outfit, as did Johnny Weissmuller as the lord of the jungle. But with an idyllic pool part of the ape man's bailiwick, there was time for an extended underwater swim scene with a nude Jane, her slinky dress whisked off by Tarzan as she drops from a limb into the water. Most agree and bemoan the fact that the underwater nymph was not O'Sullivan, rather a double.

Maureen O'Sullivan, Johnny Weissmuller, *Tarzan and His Mate* (MGM, 1934) Future Tarzan films spent more on clothing.

This then, was pre-Code Hollywood: freer, less restrictive, more natural. *Bird of Paradise* and *Tarzan and His Mate* broke all the Code's pending rules:

In the "Particular Applications" section of the Code: Section VI—Costume:

    1. *Complete nudity* is never permitted. This includes nudity in fact or in silhouette, or any lecherous or licentious notice thereof by other characters in the picture.

    2. *Undressing scenes* should be avoided, and never used save where essential to the plot.

    3. *Indecent or undue exposure* is forbidden.

Dancing costumes intended to permit undue exposure or indecent movements in the dance were forbidden.[2]

Implementation of the Production Code of 1934 changed everything. Navels and breasts were out. Tarzan and Jane covered all thigh areas. Films were not to shock or titillate or offend anyone, certainly not the religious or impressionable youths. Thus, in the United States, women's navels hardly existed prior to the sixties. Murray Schumach, chronicler of film and TV censorship, wrote, "Showing the female navel was vetoed by censors until the early 1960's. So a make-up man was ordered to plug up her navel. This looked ghastly. Whereupon a jewel was placed there and she appeared with a diamond-studded navel."[3]

Visible navels were verboten, even in costume dramas when the convention was to employ jewels to hide them in plain sight.

REAL LIFE

Ocean City, New Jersey, 1944. The city's Commissioners introduced an ordinance whereby "All persons desiring to appear in public in bathing suits shall be properly clothed in such manner as will conceal from the view of others those portions of the person as are ordinarily considered improper to expose. The torso of all such persons, including the frontal rib area shall be suitably covered." In excess of 100 men had been arrested the previous summer for wearing only trunks. The article's author suggested that apparently the chest ran down to where the ribs no longer showed.[4]

SALLY FORREST

Throughout Hollywood history, dancing girls were common in films set in the ancient world, and many a plot comes to a standstill with their dull, less than optimally erotic, often ill-choreographed or performed gyrations. But one that provided more than a boring interlude was 1955's *Son of Sinbad*, an example of many mini-epics ubiquitous at Universal, but also sometimes at RKO under the new hegemony of Howard Hughes. The leading lady in RKO's *Son of Sinbad* was Sally Forrest.

Sally Forrest might be equated with those other genuinely cute and feisty '50s leading ladies Mona Freeman, Diana Lynn, and Wanda Hendrix. In *Son of Sinbad* Sally plays Ameer. As Dale Robertson lounges amidst a plethora of harem girls, she descends a staircase and begins her lengthy routine in which her flesh is barely covered. Her back is entirely bare and her top seems to have been glued on. How else could it survive her contortions? She even accomplishes a pole dance! She wears heels. Did they have heels in the time of…Sinbad? One wonders how this escaped the ire of the censors. Apparently covering her navel was enough to mollify them.

Ms. Forrest related details about this in 2012:

> *The jewel I was wearing, in "Son of Sinbad" was amber colored, and the joke on the set was that crazy "Luden's Cough Drop" and yes, it constantly fell out. The costume at first was far more modest, but it was a Howard Hughes film and everyday there was a change in the costume. Mr. Hughes had been watching the daily's and decided to take away an item at a time. The final costume had to be glued on me, which as the days went by the chiffon (with the constant re-gluing) made me look as though I had a skin disease.*[5]

The May 25, 1955, *Boxoffice* ad [p. 23] showed a laughing Dale Robertson amongst a bevy of beauties, navels covered by their "shorts." The review on June 4, called the movie "flamboyant," "tongue-in-cheek," but pretty nonsensical. Nevertheless, "For the boys in the gallery, there probably never was so large an assemblage of cuties, curves and cleavage. The wolf whistles will, with little doubt, resound through the house and leak over into the street." It invited "slightly lurid exploitation…." All the supporting cast "had to do was look enticing, which they did in spades—and very few clothes."[6]

Howard Hughes had dabbled in film before as a producer, and he had proven to be a constant needle in the side of censors. *Son of Sinbad* provided him with new opportunity to further confound the censors. When he'd submitted the screenplay in February 1953, Joseph Breen, head of the

Sally Forrest, *Son of Sinbad* (RKO, 1955)

Production Code Administration since 1934, warned him that several scenes, particularly a harem dance, portended censorship possibilities:

> "Breasts," Breen warned, "must be fully covered at all times." Sequences in baths must not suggest nudity; the line "All these hours she's been bathing—waiting to be surprised," must be cut. So must the line, "He has harem privileges on Saturday nights." Kisses must not be open-mouthed, as indicated in the writing; there must be no bumps and grinds as in *The French Line*.

> *Hughes cut the offending lines in the script, then restored them stubbornly in the movie itself; he kept in scene after scene of semi-nudity, bumping and grinding, legs parted and raised; and all suggestions of sexual combat. It was implied that Sinbad was making love to every woman he met; and Hughes allowed a shot in which, during a lineup of the forty female thieves, one girl actually had her left breast exposed.*[7]

Although Hughes would have been contrarian anyway, by the mid-fifties Hollywood was in transition. Some of the studio moguls were dead, others retired. Admissions were drastically down, down, down. The Code had to change. Even independent producers demanded it. In 1956, there was a Code rewrite. All major taboos were lifted, except for nudity, sexual perversion, and venereal disease. It was now the *treatment* that counted.[8]

JOAN COLLINS

Far from her future as the divine bitch Alexandra Carrington throughout the eighties on TV's primetime soap opera *Dynasty*, Joan Collins, who—along with Claire Bloom, Jean Simmons, and Dana Wynter—was a ravishing British brunette filmstar of the 1950s, found her first major Hollywood film a large-scale epic from Warner Bros, *Land of the Pharaohs* (1955). It was directed by the master of most genres, Howard Hawks, and cowritten by William Faulkner, of all people. Joan played wicked Princess Nellifer, come to seduce Pharaoh. She wrote of navel issues in her autobiography, *Past Imperfect*. Director Hawks told her to cover it up because "The censor thinks navels are obscene." Collins joked to the costume designer about using a Band-

Joan Collins, *Land of the Pharaohs* (Warner Bros., 1955)
Navel covered.

Joan Collins, *Land of the Pharaohs* (Warner Bros., 1955)
Beware navel visible beneath *ur* negligee.

Aid or some Plasticine dyed her skin color, "and then I'd be navel-less, just like a big doll!" Instead, the designer had a brainstorm to use a button. A ruby was deemed best. "I looked in the mirror at the little ruby twinkling brightly in the middle of my stomach and burst into laughter. With that the ruby exploded out of its place and disappeared under a sewing machine." With Johnson's liquid adhesive, the ruby mostly stayed put, "proud and glistening, defying the censor. I thought it looked infinitely more obscene and erotic with the shiny stone drawing attention to what was meant to be unobtrusive, but everyone seemed to be satisfied, and shooting commenced." Unfortunately, good food and wine increased her midriff weight and "out plopped the dreaded red stone!"[9]

Said *Boxoffice Bookin Guide*:

> *As the Princess Nellifer, the designing femme who becomes his second wife, Joan Collins displays more of skin and sex than of talent. She delineates an ancient-history cross between Lady Macbeth and Lucrezia Borgia. What she lacks in thespian finesse, she more than balances in S. A.—and the capital letters are used advisedly. It is her contribution that will attract and please the T-shirt customers, so it is not to be overlooked—physically, that is—in exploiting the picture.*[10]

SUSAN HAYWARD

Susan Hayward, multi-Academy-Award-nominated actress, future winner for *I Want To Live!*, voted World Film Favorite by the Foreign Press in 1953 (and was more popular than Rita Hayworth, Lana Turner or Ava Gardner), was not beyond demonstrating modest terpsichorean talent—but not her navel—in a period piece. She had not been called upon to dance in 1951's *David and Bathsheba* or 1954's *Demetrius and the Gladiators*, but in 1956 she costarred as Bortai in the much derided saga of Temujin, aka Genghis Khan, played, incredibly, by John Wayne. (But remember, it's just a movie.) *The Conqueror* was another Howard Hughes RKO production, a Far Eastern *western*, and can most be appreciated for its sublime lines and horsemanship. For instance, Wayne's "I grieve that I cannot salute you as I would. I am bereft of spit!" and "You're beautiful in your wrath." Bortai used her gyrations to put Temujin off his guard before adding a sword to her repertoire and hurling it at him.

Susan Hayward, *The Conqueror* (RKO, 1956)
Midriff okay, navel not.

KIM NOVAK

In 1957's *Jeanne Eagels*, Kim Novak, capitalizing on stardom gained with the likes of 1955's *Picnic*,[11] played the stage and

Kim Novak, *Jeanne Eagels* (Columbia, 1957)

screen star of the silent era who made a few talkies before her premature death in 1929, at the age of thirty-nine. As the young Jeanne, starstruck but gaining experience in a carnival, she portrays Princess Dardanella. Despite the protestations of her impresario, Sartori (Jeff Chandler), Jeanne admits that she did indeed perform the hootchie-kootchie. She wears a somewhat revealing outfit but, alas, like Joan Collins, her navel was implanted with a jewel. Kim would reappear with and without navel obscura in the 1960s.

GINA LOLLOBRIGIDA

The Italian bombshell Gina Lollobrigida, aka "La Lollo," was a rather perfectly put together specimen. She was the epitome of symmetrical and had shapelier legs than her chief

Gina Lollobrigida, *The Beauty of the Night*
(Studios de Boulogne-Billancourt, 1952)

Italian rival. In Italian films she'd bared her midriff in *A Dog's World* (*Vita da cani*, 1950) and *The Beauty of the Night* (*Le belle della notte*, 1952).

Gina's big Hollywood period piece was *Solomon and Sheba* (1959). The Ethiopian/Arabian Queen was not beyond strutting her stuff in a revel, but she retained privacy for her bellybutton. Navel or not, Frank Leyendecker of *Boxoffice* waxed enthusiastic: "Miss Lollobrigida rates a special

Gina Lollobrigida, *Solomon and Sheba*
(Edward Small Productions/United Artists, 1959)

paragraph for her extraordinary sexy portrayal of the greatest courtesan of all time. Her face and figure are nothing less than gorgeous and her many costumes are breathtaking, particularly one sheer nightgown which displays as much of Gina's epidermis as the law permits."[12] *Films in Review* thought it neglected history but… "Fortunately, Lollo *does* take a bath."[13]

MIDRIFFS UNABASHED

"The Bikini was an atomic explosion set off by a French designer right after World War II. It has taken a decade and a half for the fallout to settle over the United States."[14]

The British annual *Film Review 1962-1963*, features a full-page, color, poolside bikini shot of Christine Kaufman, but she's pulled in her knees: no navel is visible. Nor is Tarita's in her publicity photo with Marlon Brandon on the set of *Mutiny on the Bounty*. Another full-pager has Elvis with Joan Blackman in a bikini on the *Blue Hawaii* beach. He's behind her with his arms around her waist. Thus, almost two decades after its introduction, the bikini was hesitantly and inefficiently used by U.S. filmmakers. Women in movies remained innocent of bellybuttons.

The bikini had been devised by a Frenchman, who is thought to have named it after the U.S.'s underwater atomic tests on Bikini Atoll in 1946. Test "Able" took place on July 1, 1946, while "Baker" occurred on July 25. According to journalist Hanson Baldwin, Baker was nicknamed "Bikini Helen" by Manhattan Project engineers.[15]

Continental cultural historian Patrik Alac has been one of a few to delve into the bikini's history in detail, confirming the nuclear connection and much else in *The Bikini Book*. Thus, French designer Louis Reard employed stripper Micheline Bernardini to model his world-shaking creation on July 5, 1946, at Paris's Molitor Pool, where she won the sobriquet "Most Beautiful Swimmer."[16] Couturier Jacques Heim had, that same summer, presented a two-piece outfit that covered the navel. He called it the *Atome*.[17] Alac explained:

> *Both Heim and Reard took their inspiration from political history of the era, for, during the first days of the year 1946, the newspapers were full of the most detailed reports of the atomic tests at Bikini Atoll. It was almost as if a sort of madness had taken over, in which everything was somehow linked with the bomb and its explosive power. Seductive actresses and movie stars were suddenly (and from then on) described as "Blonde bombshells on an atomic scale", suggesting that they exuded the torrid heat of sexuality with nuclear force. The word "atomic" was used as an intensifying adjective in virtually every context.*[18]

The appellation "Bikini" was a godsend for Reard "for it held within it many different connotations. It referred to a particular time and date, and yet was modern and ongoing; it evoked notions of swimming in a tropical paradise; and it came to represent a costume for a seductive beauty who revealed much of her skin with all the supposed innocence of a native Pacific islander."[19]

The first bikini was unique in terms of material as much as revealed flesh. It was not cloth, rather a collage of newspaper cuttings. "The bikini thus took every advantage of the media uproar it was bound to provoke, using every means it had in hand."[20] Alac wrote:

This lighthearted but yet explicitly knowing gesture by the designer could not emphasize more perfectly the complexity of ways in which this tiny costume would be important. Fashionable and contemporary, shocking by being the least it could possibly be, the bikini nonetheless—from the very first photo shoot, and in the most public way—set itself up as being far more than it truly was: a scrap of cloth in which a person could go swimming. It embodied fashion's ideals to be more than just an item of clothing, to tell a story, to emanate an aura of imagination and mystique around itself and around the person wearing it.[21]

Now the average kitchen-bound housewife on vacation could slip into the role of "the girl in the bikini" and transform herself "into a naïve beauty like Marilyn Monroe, or into an Amazon beauty like Ursula Andress."[22]

ADVERTISEMENTS

Corsets & Brassieres, January 1946, features an illustration of a woman in bra and panties (and heels) from Renee of Hollywood—with navel visible. "Building You Up!" Of course, these are undergarments, not beach wear.[23]

On December 21, 1949, *The New York Times* featured a large ad for General Electric's Black Daylight Television available at the local VIM Store. "The new 'Black Daylight' picture makes blacks twice as black... gives you sharper, brighter pictures." The ad was illustrated with a picture of a comely lass in a bikini, kneeling. Navel visible? No, but it would have been if the woman were standing. But such would not yet be seen in a Hollywood movie.

BRIGITTE BARDOT

Across the pond, even more cinema actresses were taking full advantage of the bikini: including the starlet Brigitte Bardot.

One perspicacious biographer opined, "Somehow Brigitte Bardot had skipped a decade. With her long blond hair and her tanned, supple, unclothed body, she had invented the sixties six years before 1963—the year in which, according to Philip Larkin, sexual intercourse was invented."[24] Bardot's celebrity "was only tangentially connected to the film roles that she took." It was a fact that outside of France, especially in English-speaking realms, people might know the title of one of her films but hardly another.[25]

And that film would hardly be *Helen of Troy*, a U.S. coproduction in which she had a small role as Andraste—not she who made Paris swoon. It was 1958's *And God Created Woman* where the mania took off and made "BB" a household name in the United States. Said *Boxoffice*, "This is the French-language import which must be credited with starting the Brigitte Bardot craze in America and, without a doubt, the provocative charms of France's little sex-kitten, as she has been aptly named, are displayed in full measure. Staid patrons might be shocked, but males will drool and attend in record-breaking numbers—as has been proven in every art house in which this has played." *Boxoffice* noted the movie's initial banning in France and some U.S. cities, and that it was a recipient of a "Condemned" rating by the Legion of Decency, "Facts which have only increased its lure for art house audiences."[26]

Films in Review had previously dismissed Bardot's *The Light Across the Street* and found only a smidgen of teasing in *Please, Mr. Balzac*. On the other hand, *And God*

Created Woman was the real thing, and FIR waxed relatively enthusiastic:

> *Here all irrelevances are discarded and there is but one pursuit: give us this day our daily bed. In full color, and against Le Tropez scenery, Bardot swims or swishes from tryst to tryst. There is a story, and it even holds water. Which is scarcely necessary. Bardot does more than Hedy did in* Ecstase *25 years ago, when film technics were cruder and current morality not so crude.*[27]

Brigitte Bardot, Cannes, 1953

THE U.S.-FRENCH FLAIR
MORE ADVERTISEMENTS

By the beginning of the next decade, bikinis were being advertised in the *New York Times*. The July 3, 1960, issue contained a large blurb for Alexander's that featured one lady in a true bikini.

They're here…our Mediterranean collection of swimsuits designed and made in France exclusively for Alexander's! Take your choice from an ocean-wide collection! On the daring side, this Bikini at $8.99. And for promenading, a matching jacket, $14.95, and slip-cover Short-Shorts, $8.99. They're exciting… they're glamorous…all spiced with the French flair…and all yours at ALEXANDER'S.

Yet, in the summer of 1960, bikinis in the United States were, in certain quarters, regarded as potentially a bust. The Bikini (capitalized then) had "not lived up to expectations" that year. In New York, Bikinis were being sold in "modest quantities... Bendel's and Bergdorf's say that some of their customers buy Bikinis, but only for wear on penthouse terraces, patios and backyards." A Lord & Taylor buyer revealed that women who had spent time overseas "buy them without a quiver. Now they're catching on among the young theatrical and artistic kids too." A Thirty-fourth Street store did well with sales, with "a heavy influx of young married women with good figures who brought their husbands along for approval. The husbands are pushing Bikinis this year, she disclosed." But would they be allowed on U.S. beaches? Regulations were few, but a Jones Beach spokesman said, "If a crowd gathers around someone playing golf in a Bikini, an officer will take action." In the Hamptons, Bikinis made their appearance "but mostly on 'artistic' types, models and Europeans." A "young matron" frowned on the item:

"If your figure is that good, it's smarter to be mysterious." Contrariwise, the English fashion model Vanessa Somers, tanning at East Hampton, said she'd taken up Bikinis five years before, in France. "When I first put one on in America, there was comment,...People were surprised, pleased and shocked. And I was embarrassed—for them. What they didn't realize is how much better the sun is if it can get to you. Of course, everything depends on one's figger."[28]

Even in 1966, Long Island beaches and clubs were questioning bikini appropriateness. "The international set hasn't raised an eyebrow over the bikini for a decade, but many women have been shy about wearing it at public beaches, and some conservative private clubs still frown on it." The Piping Rock Club in Locust Valley produced signs discouraging the garment. Yet "Making bikinis to fit the American figure has become a thriving business for... Joana Franklin and Paul Lunsford, whose no-nonsense styles are sold under the Semiramis label at Franklin Simon, Henri Bendel and Ster's Sportique shop." Contesting those who thought the bikini suitable only for skinny folks, Franklin countered, "The bikini looks best on a woman with curves."[29]

MORE CONTINENTALS

Elke Sommer, who, with Senta Berger, was a Middle Europa Teutonic voluptuosi, began making waves in such big 1963 U.S. releases as *The Prize* and *The Victors*. Like their Gallic bombshell cousin Bardot, they were used to baring their midriffs in Continental films. Eventually, Elke was permitted to do so in U.K. films, Coppertone suntan lotion ads, and September 1964, and September 1970, *Playboy* pictorials.

Elke Sommer, *Und sowas nennt sich Leben* (Alfa Film, 1961)

Elke Sommer, *Deadlier Than the Male*
(Signet Book by Henry Reymond, 1967)

THE GRETA THYSSEN STORY

Greta Thyssen, Miss Denmark 1951, parlayed her face and stunning physique into a modest TV and movie career. She was a foil for the Three Stooges, one of *Three Blondes in His Life* (1961) with Jock Mahoney, and guest actress on TV's *Perry Mason* ("The Case of the Nervous Accomplice," 1957).

Greta Thyssen, *Journey to the 7th Planet*
(American-International Pictures, 1962)

She'd worn, with distinction, negligees in *The Beast of Budapest* and *Terror is a Man*. (See Chapter 2) Then Greta Thyssen rode the winds of change and provided filmgoers with a naked navel in the Danish science fiction production *Journey to the 7th Planet* (1962). With the acting (not Greta, she was a man's imaginative figment) bordering on awful, this at least provided some excitement, especially for the male teens who must have been its target audience. *Boxoffice* identified John Agar as the only Hollywood guy in the movie, and they called the story "utterly fantastic," complimented the Cinemagic special effects, and extolled the feminine cast's looks, "including the beauteous Greta Thyssen,...who has a few screen and TV credits."[30]

Sci-fi cineaste Bill Warren felt likewise, rightfully condemning almost all the acting, and the unexplained motives of the alien "Brain," concluding it was a "boring trifle." Leading man John Agar said Thyssen deliberately tried to steal scenes.[31]

007 AND THE BOND GIRLS

Wasn't Ursula Andress's Honey Rider in *Dr. No* (1962) the first Bond girl? Not exactly. As Sylvia Trench, Eunice Gayson appeared with Sean Connery at the beginning of *Dr. No* (1962) and its follow-up, *From Russia With Love* (1963). When 007 announces himself as "Bond. James Bond" in *Dr. No*, it is to Gayson.

In *From Russia With Love*, Gayson appears in a bikini, navel visible, when she successfully goads James into putting off his meeting with M and Moneypenny. Bond films were noted for the credits sequences, and here is a belly dancer over whom the credits undulate. That terpsichorean (Lisa Nelson, aka Leila, aka Lisa Guirant) appears again in the gypsy compound sequence, this time her flesh well illuminated by the camp's fires.

But in *Dr. No*, it was the Swiss-born Ursula Andress who shocked and pleased a generation of moviegoers by making her entrance in a white bikini, exiting the island

Eunice Gayson, Sean Connery, *From Russia With Love* (United Artists, 1963)

shallows from which she'd set out to dive for conches. A belt secured a knife but did not obscure her bellybutton. A 2009 survey, of 1,000 women, ranked Andress the ultimate "bikini goddess."[32]

The James Bond films were on the cutting edge of violence and navels, if not nudity. As time passed, it became obvious that the studio wanted the largest profits possible and an R rating—even after the new MPAA Code was revised in 1968—for a bare breast would prevent teens from attending. In the meantime, there were some blatant navels, including the bikini-clad Martine Beswicke and Claudine Auger in 1965's *Thunderball*. Beauteous Molly Peters, Bond's physical therapist, showed bare reverse against frosted glass and used strategically-placed bedclothes to hide her charms in a bedroom scene. As usual, Maurice Binder acquitted himself splendidly with the title sequence, this time providing stirring, silhouetted nude swimmers.

Sean Connery, Ursula Andress, *Dr. No* (United Artists, 1962)
[publicity shot *sans* belt and knife]

TABOOS BROKEN: THE INNOVATORS, OR: SHE LOST HER NAVEL

THE DISCOVERY OF HOLLYWOOD BELLYBUTTONS

Notice the 1959 *New York Times* article "California Collections: Amusing Sportwear Designed for the Uninhibited." There are photos and in one an American lady is absolutely showing her navel.[33]

Oddly, in retrospect, Joanne Woodward—a "serious" actress if ever there was one, having won an Academy Award for Best Actress in 1957's *The Three Faces of Eve*—had posed for the camera on the Malibu Beach, in a real bikini in 1958.[34] But the chance to bare that midriff on screen didn't materialize when it should have, in *The Stripper* (1963). Balloons obscured Woodward's midsection during a "performance," and in the dressing room she wore panties that hid the navel.

Some actresses had personal peccadillos that prevented them from donning bikinis at that time. Anne Helm, a future Elvis leading lady and guest star on innumerable 1960s' TV series, reflected on her mindset during that era:

> *You want to hear how uptight I was back in the late fifties. Life magazine wanted to shoot me in a bikini and I denied… in those days that was considered pretty risqué. I don't know if it was my navel I thought about too much…it was more about being exposed with all that skin showing. How all that changed for me with all the bad girls I ended up playing. When I think about it [it] makes me smile and think how silly I was in those early years.*[35]

Joanne Woodward, 1958

THE FIRST

So who was the first *major* Hollywood leading lady to expose her midriff *on screen*? No, not Marilyn Manning in a Palm Springs pool in 1962's *Eegah!*

It was that other Marilyn: Monroe of course. Both literally and figuratively, *The Misfits* (1961) signaled the death of one Hollywood era and the beginning of another when she stumbles ashore and falls into Gable's arms.[36]

Anne Helm, *The Unkissed Bride*
(Tonylyn Productions/U.S. Films, 1966)
[by mid-decade, Helm was all in with the bikini]

Had it not been for the Code, there would have been more than a bare belly from Monroe. James Goode, on set to observe filming, conveyed the issues that were grappled with in *The Story of The Misfits*:

Arthur Miller and Frank Taylor had looked at the film of the bedroom scene; Taylor thought that the take which momentarily showed Marilyn's breast was by far the best, and wanted to keep it. Miller was undecided. They asked Marilyn, who said that it was natural. She said that the picture had no seal from the Motion Picture Association anyway, and added: "Let's get the people away from the television sets. I love to do things the censors wouldn't pass. After all, what are we all here for, just to

Marilyn Monroe, *The Misfits* (Seven Arts Productions, 1961)

stand around and let it pass us by? Gradually they'll let down the censorship—sadly probably not in my lifetime."[37]

Max Youngstein, United Artists executive, heard about the shot and said, "Let's use it! Let's do it! The time has come! This is UA's answer to television!"[38]

Cinematographer George Tomasini was concerned that a breast would cost the film money in lost earnings because censors of various stripes would condemn it. He did not know that the Motion Picture Association of America had refused a seal in advance because producer Frank E. Taylor would not originally accede to its request to, in particular, condemn the illicit sex between Gay and Roslyn.[39]

Was *The Misfits*, a hodgepodge of psychological motivations and immature characters, only important because it was the last film of its two iconic stars, Gable and Monroe? (Gable died on November 16, 1960.) That seems to have been the consensus among critics. It was not favorably reviewed. Curiously, one contemporary review was not complimentary, and not only because it considered the film an "overlong mishmash of rough action, soulsearching character analysis and psychiatric connotations. Arthur Miller, La Monroe's former husband, wrote the screenplay and, perhaps in an analytical mood, projected the femme luminary as a gal with a super-sensitive soul as well as sanctified skin. She is permitted to display too much of both."[40] Too much skin? Monroe's bare shoulders and back, or the bellybutton? Nevertheless, no one seems to have grasped the import of the bikini scene—then or later.

The New York Times review made no mention of Monroe's swimsuit.[41] Nor did *Time*, which found the film "a pseudosociological study" and "rambling, banal, loaded with logy profundities...."[42]

Out in the real world, at least in Manhattan and some other big cities, bare midriffs were on display in "belly boites," or "belly clubs." "Their burgeoning popularity may be a result of the closing of the 52nd street burlesque joints, but curiously enough their atmosphere is almost always familial—neighborhood saloons with a bit of epidermis."[43] A major agent for the dancers was one "Murat Somay, Manhattan Turk who is the Sol Hurok of the central abdomen."[44]

Subject to the still vigilant Production Code censors, Monroe's abortive *Something's Got to Give* would have escalated the exposure. But MM was a problem and was fired, and the film was shelved. Surviving clips show Marilyn nude except for towel on the edge of a swimming pool. Like that other Continental expatriate director, Otto Preminger, director Billy Wilder liked to push the envelope, as he would do shortly in *Irma La Douce* and *Kiss Me, Stupid*.

Much later, one of Monroe's biographers mentioned Monroe's bikini, but not the one from *The Misfits*, rather from *Something's Got to Give*. "Certainly she began displaying her body again, and stripped off the flesh-colored bikini she was wearing for a "skinny-dipping" scene in the film and posed nude for the first time since the beginning of her career; she was the first major movie star to pose for nude pictures on set, while a star."[45]

After Marilyn, there was a lull in midriff epidermis exploitation by major stars.

Actually, the taboo was broken again in a major Hollywood movie (filmed in Britain) but not by a *major* Hollywood actress, in 1962's *Lolita*. Vladimir Nabokov's scandalous novel became a bellweather case for freedom of expression on the screen, yet not especially for the expression of a navel.

When James Mason first meets Lolita (Sue Lyon), she is lounging in the backyard in a true, navel-revealing bikini. Note that Lyon wears a figure-covering "house-dress" by night, not a negligee. That night-dress—and the toning down of Quilty's murder—was necessary for gaining the

Production Code Seal. In the seduction scene Lolita would be attired in a "heavy flannel, long sleeved, high-necked, full-length nightgown...."[46]

Such modifications, prior to release, negated significant post-release challenges. Both the Legion of Decency and the Production Code Administration were contacted in advance, some changes made (Sue Lyon wasn't and didn't look twelve-years-old), and it received a "Special Classification" from the Legion and a "For persons over 18 only" label on all advertisements from the Motion Picture Association of America.[47]

Hope Lange might have been the next leading lady to show her navel, but there remained hesitancy in Hollywood. The poster for *Love is a Ball*, released in March of 1963, features Lange cavorting in a true bikini while other bikini-clad damsels crowd the beach. And the March 11, 1963, *Boxoffice* magazine features an ad in which Lange wears a black bikini. In the film, Lange wears a lovely collection of gowns, but sadly, though there are many gorgeously-photographed Mediterranean beachfront opportunities for cavorting, no bikini is to be seen on Hope. Research reveals that *Love is a Ball* was indeed a victim of the censors. Nine photos in *Pageant* magazine show Lange in a bikini or navel-revealing summertime ensemble.

> *Production was delayed by controversy over costumes. Designer Frank Thompson had to add two inches of material to the plunging neckline...on orders from Hollywood's blue-nosed Production Code office. And bikinis that exposed too much Hope were lengthened to show only a little promise.*[48]

Love is a Ball (Gold Medal/Oxford Productions, 1963)

SANDRA DEE: YOU BE THE JUDGE

So, following Marilyn Monroe, the next major star to show her navel on screen was…Sandra Dee! Yes, *Gidget*. One might debate whether Dee was an accomplished actress or capable of making serious films, but the Quigley Poll of movie star popularity ranked her #7 in 1960, #6 in 1961, #9 in 1962, and #8 in 1963. She showed her navel via bikini in 1963's *Take Her, She's Mine*, an amusing comedy with James Stewart as the beleaguered father no sooner getting Dee under control than her younger sister played by Charla Doherty appears in her own bikini. In the July 1963 issue of *Screen Stories* is a black-and-white photo of Dee in that bikini. The caption: "Sandra Dee wears daring bikini in 20th's "Take Her, She's Mine".

Sandra Dee, *Take Her, She's Mine* (20th Century-Fox, 1963)
[The wicker cabana chair has a long Hollywood cheesecake history.
See Susan Hayward for 1947's *They Won't Believe Me*.]

Take Her, She's Mine also plays a part in cinematic hat history, as the reader will discover later.

AIP BEACH MOVIES: HARBINGER

Eschewing the monsters and aliens that had served the studio so well as drive-in and matinee fodder since 1956, American International Pictures made a decision that upped the ante in more ways than one. On July 14, 1963, a new youth nerve was touched with *Beach Party*, the first in a wave of cheaply-made, plot-challenged sand and surf opuses.[49] Veteran actors like Vincent Price, Robert Cummings and Martha Hyer lent an air of professionalism to some of these films in which former Disney Mouseketeer Annette Funicello and pop heartthrob Frankie Avalon were usually the leads, dating, or trying to, while thwarting nefarious plans by the likes of Harvey Lembeck and Don Rickles. As the decade moved on, a plethora of *Playboy* Playmates of the Month comprised the bikinied beach bunnies kicking up sand and twisting innocently on the seashore or the beach shacks where the rock and pop groups performed. The one- and two-piece swimsuits of Sandra Dee and Yvonne Craig in Columbia's *Gidget* (1959) gave way to real bikinis in the AIP films, at least for the gals in the background, but not at first Annette. She initially willingly complied with Walt Disney's wish for the first film in the series, *Beach Party*.

Now, I see in here that all the other girls are going to be running around in bikinis, which is fine. But Annette, I want you to be different. You are different. I would simply like to request that you not expose your navel in the film.

*"Mr. Disney, that's not a problem. Of course, I won't," I replied. And it wasn't; at least not for me. I wore a bikini around my own pool at home, but never in public. So I was happy to comply with Mr. Disney's request.*⁵⁰

When a producer or director requested that Annette drop the prohibition, she said, "This is something I chose to do and will do." She added, "I was quaking inside, but I refused to let myself be bullied into doing what everyone else was doing. I think this is part of my character—both onscreen and off—that audiences sensed and responded to."⁵¹

As Sister Irmenelda informed her Wilmington, Delaware Padua High School, class, Annette would never wear something like that. Annette wore one-pieces or two-pieces with netting over the top. But…in *Bikini Beach*, the third "beach" movie, Annette wears, heavens, a genuine, bellybutton-revealing bikini.

John Ashley, Jody McCrea, Annette Funicello, Frankie Avalon, *Bikini Beach* (American International Pictures, 1964)

Ghost in the Invisible Bikini (American International Pictures, 1966) Note Susan Hart's navel airbrushed out of poster.

Sue Hamilton, aka *Playboy*'s April 1965 Playmate Sue Williams, *Dr. Goldfoot and the Bikini Machine* (American International Pictures, 1965) A bikini for the ages.

Other studios followed AIP's lead. On August 5, 1964, Columbia released *Ride the Wild Surf*, which proved to be one of, if not the, best of this tide. Navels were shown by the three feminine leads, including Susan Hart, moving over from AIP before returning for *Pajama Party, Dr. Goldfoot and the Bikini Machine* and *Ghost in the Invisible Bikini*. Eden could show navel here but not on the forthcoming TV series *I Dream of Jeannie*.

Susan Hart, Shelley Fabares, Barbara Eden,
Ride the Wild Surf (Columbia, 1964)

Another beach bunny was Gail Gerber, aka Gail Gilmore. She appeared in 1965's *Girls on the Beach* and *Beach Ball*: "I had come from Toronto by way of Montreal to escape the Canadian winter, and bought my first bikini in Montreal when they were invented. I would rinse it out and hang it on the patio to dry. I had no hang-ups because I was trained as a ballet dancer, and lived in tights and leotard. We supplied our own wardrobe for those movies."[52]

Gail Gerber, *Girls on the Beach* (Levin Bros./Paramount, 1965)

In addition to bikinis, the enduring legacy of '60s "beach movies" from AIP and other studios were the sets performed by current and up and coming singers and groups. These included James Brown, the Hondells, the Del-Tones, Little Stevie Wonder, the Animals, the Beach Boys, Lesley Gore, the Supremes, the Kingsmen, the Walker Brothers, the Four Seasons, and the Righteous Brothers.

ELVIS: WHAT'S UP WITH THAT?

One might expect—or not, what with Elvis's clean-cut image (well, not so clean cut as Pat Boone)—that his shore-side frolics would feature some leading-lady navels. Not in 1961's *Blue Hawaii*, however. Although he brings home from his military tour of duty in Europe a French swimsuit, a bikini of course, it obscures Joan Blackman's bellybutton. The young ladies he coaches in surfing techniques all wear one-pieces. Although Nancy Walters's Ellie tells him "I don't wear britches!" and sports a peignoir, all is chaste, with nothing seen between thigh and neck.

Despite setting up shop on the Florida beach in 1962's *Follow That Dream*, Elvis's leading lady, Anne Helm, never wears a swimsuit. In *Girls! Girls! Girls!* that same year, voluptuous Stella Stevens, having shown some skin as *Playboy*'s January 1960 Playmate of the Month, gets to wear... a one-piece.

Times were changing, however. In 1965's *Tickle Me*, Elvis's femme lead Jocelyn Lane and others at the dude ranch pool were outfitted with true bikinis.

In 1966's *Paradise, Hawaiian Style*, Julie Parrish showed navel between blouse and pants. Susanna Leigh went the full bikini route.

There was backtracking in 1968's *Live a Little, Love a Little*. Femme lead Michele Carey, who earlier that year wore a bikini in *The Sweet Ride*, was back in a one-piece. What was up with that? 1968 was the year the new rating system took effect, and more than a navel was acceptable to the MPAA.

Jocelyn Lane, *Tickle Me* (Allied Artists, 1965)

MAJOR STAR MIDRIFFS

NATALIE WOOD

What of the major Hollywood female stars? Marilyn had worn that bikini in 1961's *The Misfits* but had not started a trend. It would have been entirely appropriate for Natalie Wood to be the next mainstream star after Monroe to display a navel on screen. In *Gypsy* (1962) Natalie played an allegedly no-talent young lady who became legendary striptease artiste Gypsy. During those vaudeville segments she gets down to a top and bottom with a large stretch of flesh in between. However, there in the few seconds she displays this while curtains close or open, it appears the costumers have coated her midsection with glitter or plastered on sparkled netting. Contrast this with the still photos in which she presents a totally bare belly.

This belly bowdlerization of course was not new. Although the Production Code and the Legion of Decency were losing the war against freedom of exposure, producers remained primed to trim nude scenes of Natalie Wood in *Splendor in the Grass* (1961), Kim Novak in *Of Human Bondage*, Carroll Baker in *The Carpetbaggers* (1964), and Elizabeth Taylor in *The Sandpiper* (1965). *The Americanization of Emily* (1964) and *The Cincinnati Kid* (1965) were also in this category.[53] Nudity or even navel would certainly have given some needed zip to such rather dull and shopworn soap operas as *Carpetbaggers* and *Sandpiper*—the latter only enlivened by Charles Bronson's sublime request of Richard Burton's clergyman: "Ya know, Reverend, I've always had a yen to ask some qualified person a few questions about the virgin

Natalie Wood, *Gypsy* (Warner Bros., 1962)

birth." The same criticism holds for *Bondage*, which at least featured Novak's profoundly beautiful back.

It wasn't until 1966 that Natalie Wood was able to show her midriff in the caper comedy *Penelope*. At that moment, there was no penalty for baring her belly, wearing a shortie

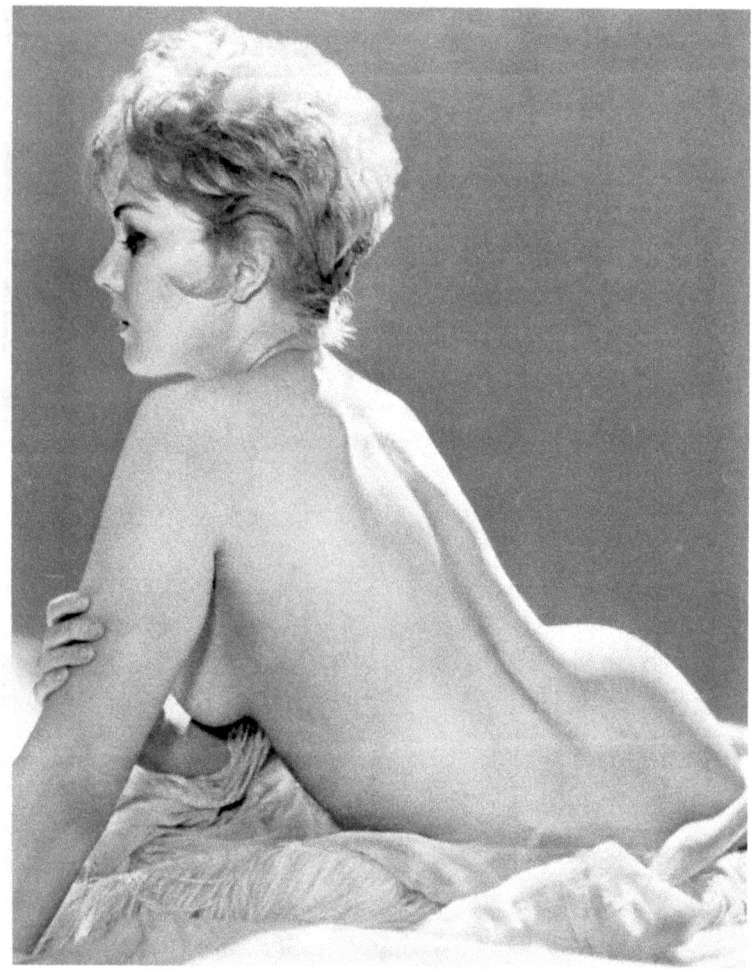

Kim Novak, *Of Human Bondage* (MGM/Seven Arts, 1964)

nightie, and, in bra and panties, getting chased around a room by Jonathan Winters.

REEL TO REAL CHALLENGES

A kick in the belly of movie censorship occurred in August 1963. Jayne Mansfield, blonde film sexpot second only to

Natalie Wood, *Penelope* (MGM, 1966)

Marilyn Monroe in celebrity status and star of *The Girl Can't Help It* and *Will Success Spoil Rock Hunter?*, went bare in *Promises.....Promises!* There was no MPAA rating for this unashamed "nudie" in which Mansfield prominently displayed her breasts and belly. Thus Jayne warrants mention

Shirley MacLaine, *Irma La Douce*
(Mirisch Corporation, 1963)

as a groundbreaker in film; another nail in the coffin of the now hoary Motion Picture Production Code.

Beyond the realm of film, bikinis, despite the premature reports of their demise in the States, were legitimized by *Sports Illustrated* on January 20, 1964. With a bikini-clad

Babette March on the cover, this was the first of *SI*'s soon to be famous special swimsuit issues.

MACLAINE VS. NOVAK

And then came Shirley MacLaine. She ranked #7 in the Quigley 1964 poll and was a "serious" actress, having received Best Actress Academy Award nominations for *Some Came Running* (1958), *The Apartment* (1960) and *Irma La Douce* (1963). The All-American Screen Favorites Poll—of newspaper and magazine editors, theater owners, domestic and international radio and television correspondents, and National Screen Council members—ranked MacLaine #2 in 1964. Sandra Dee was #6.[54]

One might think Billy Wilder's *Irma La Douce* (1963) would permit an unadorned navel. The story concerns a Parisian prostitute (MacLaine) and her affair with a gendarme (Jack Lemmon). But Hollywood censors were still enforcing their strictures. *Look* Magazine ran a cover story on a bolder Hollywood but, "'It's a good thing we're having so much fun making it,' goes the fixed jest there, 'because it will never be seen anyplace else.'" But it was and became a hit though the ad warned, "THIS PICTURE IS FOR ADULTS ONLY".

Look further commented:

The directing of the film, or the matter of choosing when and where not to leer while speaking double entendres, is attended to by Billy Wilder, the jack-of-two-trades who wrote the script with I. A. L. Diamond. Wilder had previously guided the MacLaine-Lemmon pairing through The Apartment (same scriptwriters) to wide-spread praise and vast box-office receipts. That venture proved that a little impropriety pays, and the supposition now must be that a larger serving of the same will pay more....The feeling most prevalent around the studio is that this movie about a girl who makes love for a living will be at least racy enough to pull crowds, though hopefully not so racy that the keepers of the Production Code Seal might withhold it.[55]

Despite the risqué nature of the film, and a smidgen of cleavage, MacLaine does not show navel. Almost, but not quite. It was not yet 1964, when this free spirit's bellybutton would get the green light, not a green emerald.

MacLaine was pictured all spiffed up on the cover of *The Saturday Evening Post*, November 30, 1963, promoting the future release of *What a Way to Go!* That film, released on May 12, 1964, was a kind of last gasp for Hollywood glamour and a certain kind of frivolous storyline: MacLaine as Louisa May Foster, who through no fault of her own marries multiple times because each husband (Paul Newman, Dean Martin, Robert Mitchum, and Gene Kelly) becomes obsessed with some scheme or vocation and in its pursuit kicks the bucket. Lounging around the pool, battling ennui, the ever unconventional MacLaine wore a real bikini. One wonders if the censors would have axed the scene if this hadn't been a comedy? The June 1, 1964, issue of *Boxoffice* featured a full-page ad that was MacLaine in that bikini. "In New York...Chicago...Philadelphia...Washington... Los Angeles...Boston! Watch 20th's great attraction GO everywhere Mid-June."

MacLaine bested another Hollywood luminary in navel revelation by half a year. In the film whose outraged reviews virtually stopped director Billy Wilder's fabulous career in

Shirley MacLaine, *What a Way to Go!*
(20th Century-Fox, 1964)

its tracks, Kim Novak paid tribute to the past and prefigured the future. In *Kiss Me, Stupid*, released December 22, 1964, Novak played Polly the Pistol, the trailer tramp of Climax, Nevada. (Imagine anyone looking like Kim Novak being found in such a dump!) She sported an abbreviated vest and a fringed skirt, between which a wide expanse of flesh was visible. Yet, as with Joan Collins and Gina Lollobrigida before her, a jewel was inserted into her bellybutton. But... late in the film, Kim sneezes and pops out that jewel. The camera goes in close on Kim's belly. Then, crawling around

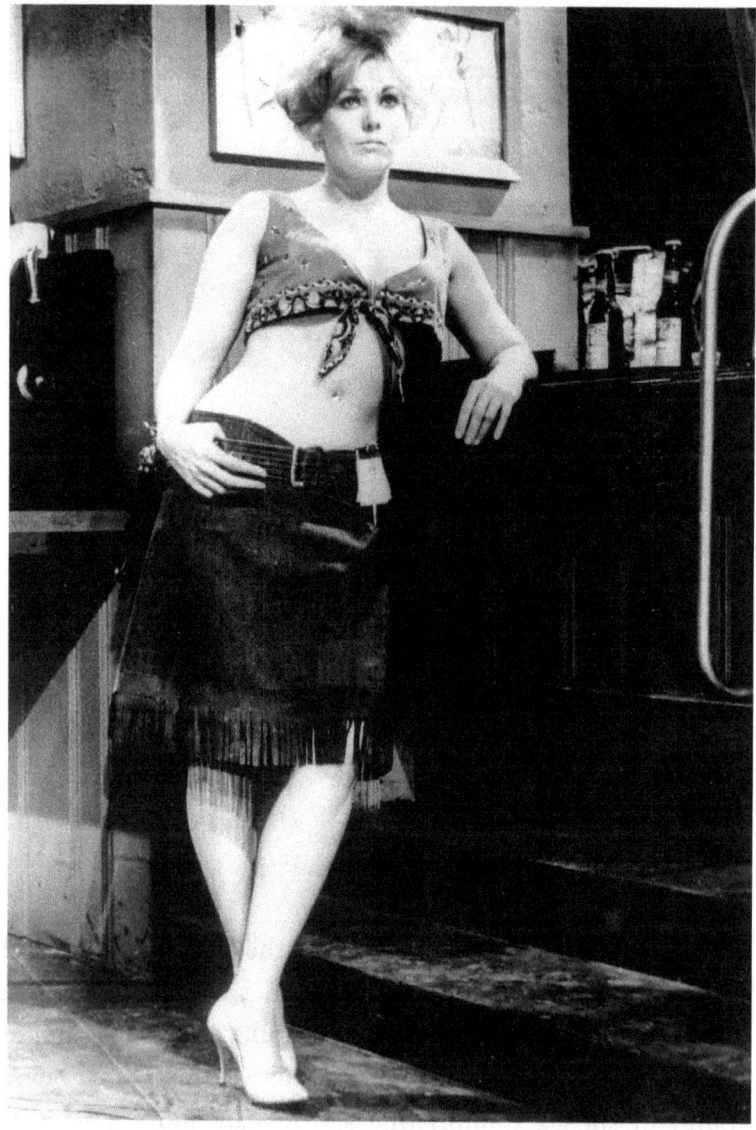

Kim Novak, *Kiss Me, Stupid* (Lopert/United Artists, 1964)

to find her jewel, she exclaims to Ray Walston, "I lost my navel."[56] Ironically, the window card for the film airbrushed

Kiss Me, Stupid (Lopert/United Artists, 1964)

out Novak's bellybutton even though the copy extols a girl's navel as "of great sentimental value."

Perhaps the same *Boxoffice* magazine reviewer of *The Misfits* three years previously critiqued this one, too. This Wilder and I. A. L. Diamond effort "almost comes a cropper with his latest, a feeble, often tasteless and over-acted farce-comedy. However, Wilder's fame and the marquee names of Kim Novak and Dean Martin will insure good box-office returns, although some vulgarities in the situations and dialog make it 'Adults Only' fare."[57] One conjectures that such criticism would be tempered if the film had been made and released later in the decade. Few moviemakers or anyone else could have been expecting the imminent convergence of civil rights, feminism, massive anti-Vietnam War protests, and the transformation of the Production Code.

Keeping pedal to the medal, Shirley MacLaine outdid her navel exposure in *What a Way to Go!* when *John Goldfarb, Please Come Home* was released on March 24, 1965. Like *Kiss Me, Stupid*, this was widely panned, but not for vulgarity and indecency, rather for stupidity in its tale of the Notre Dame college football team playing a game in Arabia with journalist MacLaine posing as a harem girl to get the story. Said *Film Annual*:

> *Loose-jointed, pretty crazy comedy which pokes fun at the U.S. Foreign [sic] Department and anything else which takes its fancy in a rather thin but complicated story about an Arab King who offers a challenge to America's Notre Dame college football team, a wrong-way aviator who should be spying over Russia but is in fact coaching the king's team of whirling dervishes, and the girl reporter who once smuggled into the harem finds it less easy to smuggle herself out—untouched?*[58]

Novak, too, would display more bare midriff as the decade continued, especially in *The Legend of Lylah Clare* (1968) and *The Great Bank Robbery* (1969). The latter film received an M

John Goldfarb, Please Come Home
(20th Century-Fox, 1965)

rating from the MPAA, which perplexed both producer and director. They'd wanted a G, even though "the film features (1) Kim Novak, clad in nothing but a few strategically-placed daisies, atop a horse, (2) a scene of Miss Novak and

Clint Walker undressing, preparatory to lovemaking, while 'high' on peyote, and (3) several spicy logisms,..."59

Gabriele Tinti, Peter Finch, Kim Novak, *The Legend of Lylah Clare* (Associates & Aldrich/MGM, 1968)

THE COPPERTONE GALS

Look back at Stella Stevens's 1963 Coppertone ad. She wore a one-piece swimsuit. Elke Sommer's Coppertone ad appearances mirrored changing times. In 1965, when promoting *The Art of Love*, she wore a bikini but hid her navel with her arm. In 1966, promoting *The Oscar*, she showed off her midsection. To plug Coppertone and the 1967 film *Don't Make Waves*, a bikinied Sharon Tate lay on her back on a surfboard. But in 1968, Mitzi Gaynor, whose last feature film had been 1963's *For Love or Money* but who was setting records and garnering critical acclaim with her Vegas dance review and TV specials, did a Coppertone ad. Mitzi's arm obscured what might have been a bare bellybutton and also hid her cleavage.

Playboy Playmate Anne Randall (May, 1967), who would achieve a measure of success on TV (*Streets of San Francisco, Mod Squad, Barnaby Jones, Cannon, Love, American Style*) and as the heroine of action-exploitation movie *Stacey* (1973), was featured in Coppertone suntan lotion ads in 1968. For the shoot on a Southern California beach she was "picked up and delivered to the set by a production driver." In the print ad she wore a white bikini with navel visible. Anne thinks the bikini belonged to Coppertone but that they gave it to her after the filming. The "Victrola" to which she was presumably jiving was actually mute.[60] Anne also did a Coppertone TV ad.

> *They shot it first with a nude-colored bandage over my navel. I asked the director what the bandage was for. He said, "They don't allow navels on television." I told him I thought it was crazy because all it was going to accomplish was to make me look like a freak. As a result, they shot it TWO WAYS, with a navel and without a navel. I didn't think anything of it when the version with a navel appeared on television. There is not a*

person on this planet that is without a navel! Also I was chosen for many reasons, but one of them was that I had an "inny." I've been told I was the first belly button ever to appear on television, as it turned out. All I did was to question the use of a bandage and history was made.[61]

Ann-Margret, *The Swinger* (Paramount, 1966)
Who are *those* guys?!

ANN-MARGRET

Singer-dancer-actress Ann-Margret began her film career after attracting attention in George Burns's Las Vegas show. Her movie debut was *Pocketful of Miracles* (1961). Another significant ingénue role in *State Fair* (1962) followed, and more important assignments in *Bye Bye Birdie* (1963) and, with Elvis, in *Viva Las Vegas* (1964). In keeping with the changing times, her characters and attire became sexier as the decade progressed. Ads for 1965's *Bus Riley's Back in Town* in *Boxoffice* pictured her in a bikini, navel prominent.[62] Photos for an extensive interview in the June 1965 issue of *Sound Stage* showed a wide and bare midriff betwixt what could pass for a vinyl top and vinyl slacks but was probably Lycra. "I dig clothes. But wild."[63] In 1966's *The Swinger* her attire left little to the imagination.

RAMIFICATIONS FOR TV

Despite playing an exotic genie, Barbara Eden was not allowed to show her navel in TV's *I Dream of Jeannie*, which ran from 1965 to 1970. Although she wrote that her navel was visible whenever she raised her arms, nobody noticed. "Famously, I was never allowed to expose my belly button on the show."[64] There was a scheme to reveal her navel on *Rowan and Martin's Laugh-In*, and Barbara wanted to accede to the requests from U.S. soldiers overseas, but NBC would have none of it.[65] Even when there were episodes filmed on the Hawaiian beaches, Barbara had to wear a one-piece.[66]

Curiously, Mary Ann Mobley, Miss America of 1959, who became an actress in films and on TV, showed her navel in the two-part "Old Man Out" episodes of *Mission:*

Impossible, October 8 and 15, 1966. Perhaps it was allowed because she was masquerading as a circus trapeze artiste.

STELLA STEVENS

Stella Stevens had already begun a film career (chorus girl in *Say One for Me*, Apassionata Von Climax in *Li'l Abner*) when she became the January 1960 *Playboy* Playmate after the magazine's prospectors scanned "the hoopla hills of Hollywood for Playmates and we came upon fair Stella, deemed her delightful to behold, and invited her to pose for our famous center spread."[67] In her centerfold and the 1961 Playmate Calendar, Stella revealed only her posterior. But, in the May 1965 and January 1968 *Playboy* pictorials, her navel was on display along with her other fleshly charms. (Whoever said Stella was one of the ten most photographed women of the '60s was probably correct.)

Daliah Lavi, Stella Stevens, Dean Martin, *The Silencers* (Columbia, 1966)

The 1966 spy spoof *The Silencers* featured Dean Martin as ICE (Intelligence/Counter/Espionage) agent Matt Helm, master of women and enemy agents. Suspecting Gail Hendricks (Stevens, with red rather than her normal blonde tresses) of nefarious activities though she's a dumb cluck, Helm throws her into a room and after she gets up, rips off her dress, leaving her in bra, panties, and stockings.[68] Is Helm looking for spyware or ogling cleavage and belly? Perhaps in a back-handed, unintentional way it *was* women's liberation!

DORIS DAY

The Glass Bottom Boat was perennial film favorite Doris Day's 1966 comedic entry. Early in the film, Day finds herself masquerading as a mermaid for tourists. Observing her underwater, one might *claim* a glimpse of navel. Later, in a fantasy sequence, she mimics Garbo as Mata Hari in Javanese or Balinese dancer's attire. Even though it's 1966, like Garbo, Day's navel is covered by a large jewel—in the print that audiences see. It appears that the filmmakers, trying to get "with it," chickened out. In costume tests, Day's unadorned navel is front and center.

HAMMER MIDRIFFS, OR: RAQUEL WELCH, EXEMPLAR

On the British Isles, midriffs were getting their due in the films of Hammer Studios—since 1956, an eminently successful purveyor of science fiction (*The Quatermass Xperiment, X the Unknown*), gothic horror in color (*The Curse of Frankenstein, Horror of Dracula, The Mummy*), and prehistoric rambles (*Prehistoric Women*, aka *Slave Girls*, 1967).

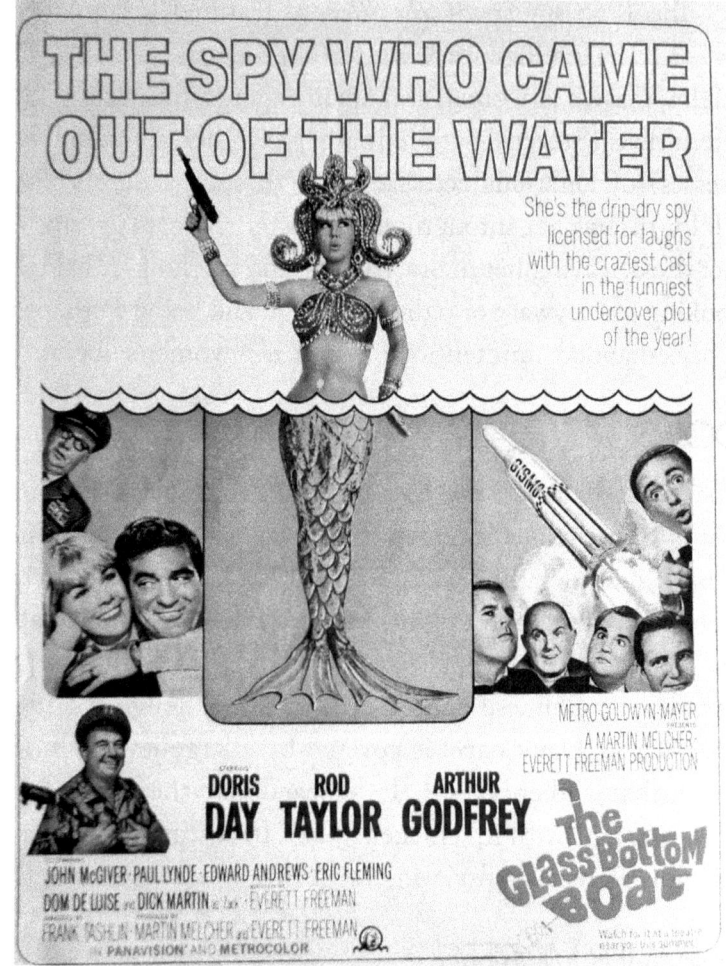

The Glass Bottom Boat (MGM, 1966)

August 1966 *Playboy* Playmate Susan Denberg showed her navel in *Frankenstein Created Woman*.

The studio's films were just as popular in the U.S. and one of them featured an actress in what became, though it was presumably animal skin and fur, one of the decade's iconic bikinis: *One Million Years B.C.* The wearer: Raquel Welch.

NAVEL ART

Prehistoric Women (Hammer, 1967)

Released in Europe in 1966, it reached North American shores in 1967. *Variety* considered the leading lady more saleable than the dinosaurs and the spectacle. Apparently there had been industry scuttlebutt about the new sex symbol, for "at last, the nubile Raquel Welch is on view. Till more seen in stills than screened, Miss Welch here gets little opportunity to prove herself as an actress but she is certainly there in the looks department."[69] *Boxoffice* gave Welch the cover on its February 6, 1967, issue with three interior pages plugging the movie. "First there was man… woman … and beast… THIS IS THE WAY IT WAS"

Here, thirty-four years after Dolores Del Rio exposed her belly as Luana in *Bird of Paradise*, Raquel Welch, in an even more primitive environment, revealed hers. What was *her* character's name? Loana!

Raquel Welch, *One Million Years B.C.* (Hammer, 1966)

MPAA RATING SYSTEM

As we have seen, by the 1960s, the Production Code of 1934 was in dire need of change—or termination. Clever filmmakers like Billy Wilder had always employed wit and style to circumvent its censorious provisions. Not so far back, in 1956, the Code had been based on these General Principles:

> 1. No picture shall be produced which will lower the moral standards of those who see it. Hence the sympathy of the audience shall never be thrown to the side of crime, wrong-doing, evil or sin.
> 2. Correct standards of life, subject only to the requirements of drama and entertainment, shall be presented.
> 3. Law—divine, natural or human—shall not be ridiculed, nor shall sympathy be created for its violation.[70]

Even on the eve of events in movies and real life that would necessitate drastic changes in film censorship, some organizations took a conservative tack and were for *strengthening* the Code. In 1961, the American Congress of Exhibitors, Theatre Owners of America, and Allied States Association urged the Motion Picture Association of America to bolster interpretation as well as application of the Production Code.[71]

Nevertheless, these organizations were fighting a losing battle. By the second half of the decade, a real transformation, even liberalization of the Code was needed. In part, this was to circumvent governmental interference. To protect children from the increasing sex, nudity, violence, and foul language on the screen in both Hollywood films and imported ones, Senator Margaret Chase Smith of Maine proposed a Federal classification system.[72] Can one presume the nudity alluded to was Jayne Mansfield in *Promises, Promises?* There was as yet no real nudity in mainstream Hollywood films.

Despite the imminent new MPAA system, the National Catholic Office for Motion Pictures was expected to merely modify, not end its own rating policy. NCOMP would continue to "indicate the age suitability of every film we see."[73]

When the new rating system took effect in November 1968, seventy-two features were rated by the MPAA.[74]

Conflicts arose immediately. Some wondered why the lesbian-themed *The Fox* received the R rather than the X rating, as the latter would have stopped those under seventeen from attending. And what of *Birds in Peru*, the very steamy French film with Jean Seberg? It got an X, but there was no actual nudity.[75]

THE GOLDEN AGE OF THE R RATING

The new Motion Picture Code and Rating Plan took effect on November 1, 1968. Jack Valenti, president of the Motion Picture Association of America, labeled exhibitors key to enforcement.[76] Certainly filmmakers were eager to test the plan's boundaries. Navels and nudity were "in." Swinging Britain was eminently prepared and took advantage of this *movement*, what with Judy Geeson and Vanessa Howard in *Here We Go Round the Mulberry Bush* (1968); Anne Heywood in *The Fox* (1968); Pamela Franklin in *The Night of the Following Day* (1968) and *The Prime of Miss Jean Brodie* (1969); and American *Playboy* Playmate Connie Kreski in Anthony Newley's *Can Heironymous Merkin Ever Forget Mercy Humppe and Find True Happiness?* (1968). From France came *Barbarella* (1968) with Jane Fonda showing skin during the credits in a famous zero-gravity striptease. It took a smidgen longer in the U.S. for outright nudity in mainstream features. *The Night They Raided Minsky's* (1968) featured a Britt Ekland double, baring her breasts,[77] followed by bosom-baring-Brit Susannah York in *The Killing of Sister George*. In *Beyond the Valley of the Dolls* (1970), former *Playboy* centerfolds Dolly Read and Cynthia Myers, plus Angel Ray and others were periodically nude, although were filmed in a herky-jerky fashion as if the filmmakers or studio feared the consequences of lingering on flesh. There was JoAnna Cameron in *B. S. I Love You* (1971) and *Pretty Maids All in a Row* (1971); Jo Ann Harris in *The Beguiled* (1971); Donna Mills in *Play Misty for Me* (1971); Pamela Franklin in *Necromancy* (1972); Cybill Shepherd in *The Last Picture Show* (1972); and Stella Stevens, back and displaying in *Slaughter* (1972).

Violence, nudity, and profanity—including the "N" word, became commonplace. In 1969, *The Wild Bunch* carried pistol, rifle, shotgun, machinegun, and grenade violence to a new level. Unofficially beginning with 1971's *Shaft*, "blaxploitation" gave vent to language and sentiments not previously heard on the screen. (Richard Roundtree: "You ain't so white, baby!")

The display of nudity continued through the early 1970s with Ingrid Pitt, *The Vampire Lovers* (1970) and *Countess Dracula* (1971); Mimsy Farmer, *Road to Salina* (1970); Jean Seberg, *Macho Callahan* (1970); Linda Hayden, *The Blood on Satan's Claw* (1971); the Collinson twins, *Twins of Evil* (1971); Yutte Stensgaard, *Lust for a Vampire* (1971); Jenny Agutter, *Walkabout* (1971); Jane Fonda, *Klute* (1971); Pam Grier, *Coffy* (1973); Ahna Capri, *Enter the Dragon* (1973).

Even a few actors got into the act, including Omar Sharif in *Mackenna's Gold* (1969), and Oliver Reed and Alan Bates in *Women in Love* (1969). The Reed-Bates wrestling match was not the only nude confrontation of males. Yes, folks, the rumors are true: an in-the-buff Leonard Nimoy wrestled with Yul Brynner in the 1970 western *Catlow*.

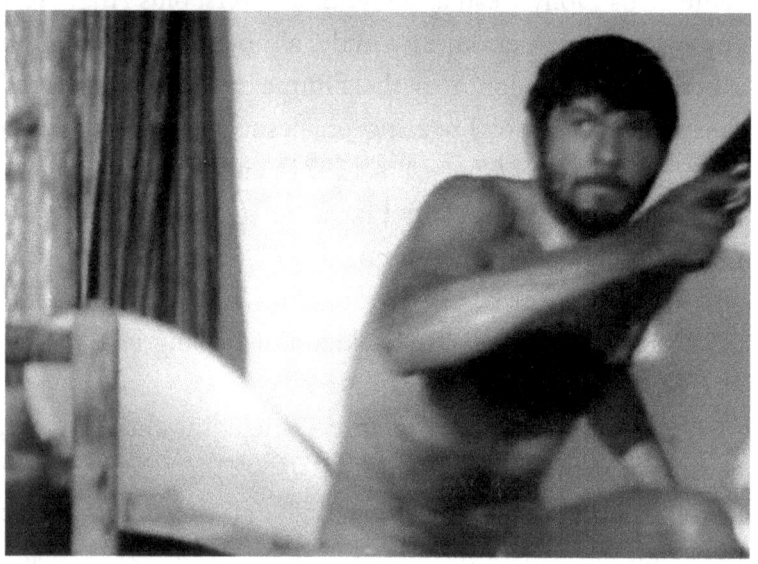

Leonard Nimoy in *Catlow* (MGM, 1970)

It didn't take long for backlash or, perhaps, quibbling. Favorably reviewing most of *Here We Go Round the Mulberry Bush*, a critic nevertheless complained, "The film has the usual 'wild party' scene, and even a nude one. Both are becoming a bore."[78]

ADS, BOOKS AND MAGAZINES

Was there a correlation between film and printed visual literary freedom? For truly sexist ads, see those for Griffin

Microshine Stain Boot Polish—especially the 1957 ones that appeared in *Playboy*. The ads featured genuine bikinis and see-through nighties.

Discounting such "men's" or "girly" magazines, even many pulp paperbacks and genre periodicals of the 1950s and 1960s were bereft of bare bellies. Yet, in 1949, the Dell paperback edition of historical novelist Edison Marshall's *Yankee Pasha* had been ahead of the curve. Next to our square-jawed hero, spyglass in hand, frigate in the background, stands an alluring blonde, all bedecked in frills and furbelows. Her bosoms are hardly obscured and more to our point, there is a wide expanse of midriff with navel prominent.

Yankee Pasha by Edison Marshall (Dell, 1947)

By 1964, the same year that Shirley MacLaine and Kim Novak bared their bellies on screen, bikinied sexpots became acceptable on paperbacks. Take, for example, Charles X. Wolffe's "Never Before Published" *Resort Girls*: A fully fleshed, bikinied and windswept brunette graces the cover for this Beacon publication: "A SHOCKING AND UNASHAMED NOVEL ABOUT HOT-BLOODED WOMEN WHO ABANDON EVERYTHING FOR TWO WEEKS OF UNINHIBITED SEX."

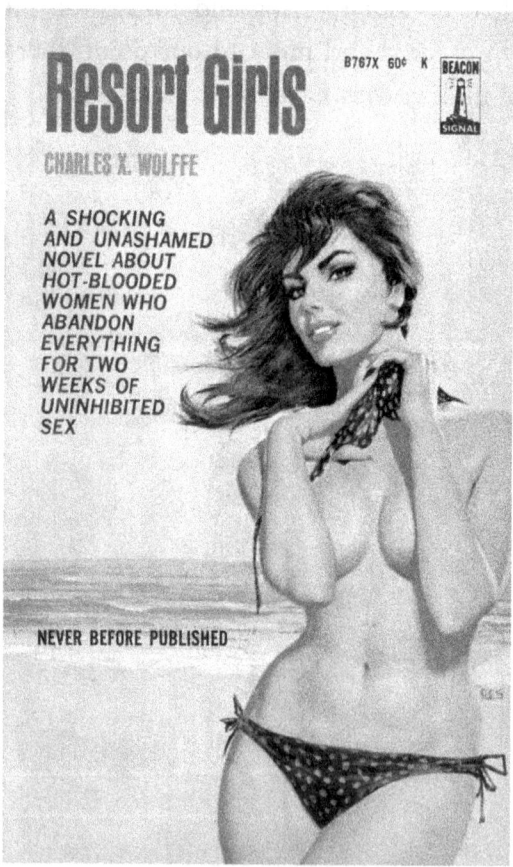

Resort Girls by Charles X Wolffe
(Beacon Hill Press, 1964; cover illustration by Res)

The Night They Raided Minsky's
(United Artists, 1968) Frank Frazetta art.

In the realm of fantastic and exotic literature, navel appearance on paperback covers paralleled their display on screen. Frank Frazetta, iconic illustrator of the fantastic, including voluptuous women, provided heroines in animal skin bikinis on the covers of *The Lost Continent* (1963), *Savage Pellucidar* (1963) and *Land of Terror* (1964). Pubescent males ate these up. *Rogue Roman* from Fawcett Books (1965) had barely clothed, muscled men and well-proportioned women. Frazetta also provided the belly-baring Cija, Princess of Atlantis, on the cover of the Paperback Library version of Jane Gaskell's *The Serpent* (1968). For Lancer Books, he did the cover for Robert E. Howard's *Conan the Adventurer* (1966). Beside that becoming-eponymous barbarian from the Hyperborian Age standing atop a mound of bodies and skulls was a fully nude maiden. Frazetta did the cover for the comic *Vampirella*, September 1, 1969, as well as *Eerie*'s "Egyptian Queen" that September. Also from Frazetta came such film posters with bikinied and scantily-clad babes as *What's New Pussycat?* (1965), *The Busy Body* (1967) and *The Night They Raided Minsky's* (1968).

Another admired fantasy illustrator, Jeff Jones, drew midriff-revealing females on the covers of the paperbacks *The City* (1968) also by Jane Gaskell, *The Curse of Rathlaw* by Peter Saxon (1968), *Thongor and the Wizard of Lemuria* by Lin Carter (1969), and *The Sword of Morning Star* (1969) by Richard Meade.

NATALIE WOOD REDUX

Recall that Natalie Wood showed bare midriff in the production stills (but not the finished film) for 1962's *Gypsy*, but that in 1966 she was permitted to show a navel in a modish slacks and top outfit in *Penelope*. Evolution continued, and the Code changed in 1968. So, in 1969, it was time for *Bob & Carol & Ted & Alice*—a humorous film essay on infidelity—which allowed Natalie to wear a bikini *and* bra and panties.

Natalie Wood, *Bob & Carol & Ted & Alice* (Columbia, 1969)

FULL CIRCLE

Now, in the first decade of the new century, bared bellybuttons are commonplace, in Western society and on screen. Yet... obscurantism raises its head again. Navel shields and jewelry are used by young and mature women alike, to both enhance and camouflage the navel. Muse on the increasing willingness of coeds and other young women to bare their entire torsos for beads (and the public) at New Orleans's Mardi Gras—since the 1970s, no less. Cameras will capture the event, the web will display for all. What are we to make of this coexistence of exhibiting with obscuring? It is perhaps more evidence of a schizophrenic society: on one side, the anorexic and bulimic denying and attenuating the flesh, on the other, the unashamed or, in some instances, juvenile display of skin and curves. How much is caused by societal schizophrenia, how much by internal... *self-loathing*? But we become too serious. It might merely be public intemperance. Let's move on to another movie cliché that went the way of all flesh: negligees.

CHAPTER 2
NIGHTTIME NYMPHS: THE GOLDEN AGE OF NEGLIGEES

"It's hard to imagine anyone in a negligee speaking to Raymond Burr. But I guess in movies everything's possible!"
—Warren Hope email, Dec. 8, 2010, on the *Affair in Havana* lobby card featuring Sara Shane and Burr

NEGLIGEE DEFINITION AND ORIGIN

The definition of negligee or, in French, *néglig*ée, is as loose as the actual garment. It's a sheer dressing gown, a housecoat, a wrapper for women, flowing, often with

Affair in Havana (Allied Artists, 1957)

lace trim. It's revealing. The French word *négligé* connotes carelessness. In that sense, it became the perfect garment for female movie characters ascending staircases to mysterious upper floors in search of answers, holding a candelabra over a spouse to determine mortality, slipping from the sheets to pursue or be pursued by lunatics, ghosts or a shrieking skull. Careless indeed were these characters. Careless also in the sense of attire that enticed and lured.

When were negligees first worn in movies? It's difficult to say. How does one distinguish between housecoats, robes, silken night attire and what would come to be the traditional negligee?

Not surprisingly, movie heroines in nighttime attire wandered dark corridors throughout Hollywood history. See

Elyse Knox in *The Mummy's Tomb* (1942) and Gail Russell in *The Uninvited* (1944). But sometimes their nightdresses might be more voluminous than what we might desire in a negligee. They might be *dressing gowns*.

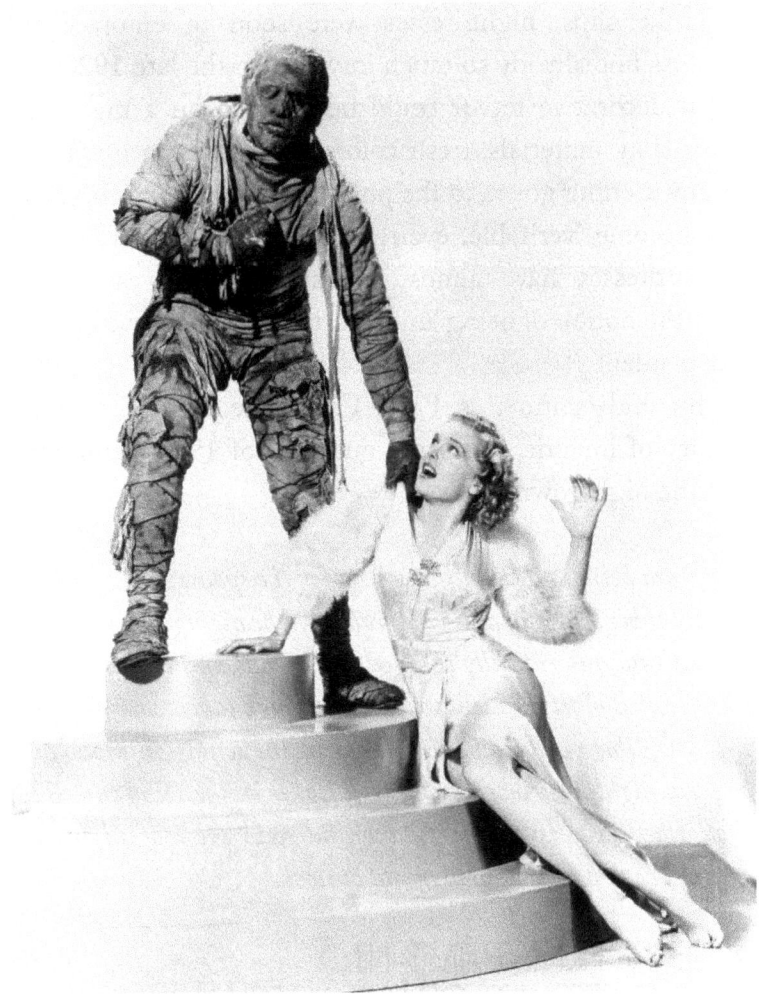

Elyse Knox, *The Mummy's Tomb* (1942)
Even back then, monsters favored scream queens in nighttime attire.

In the 1930s, "The new, prettified nightdresses and negligees, and even, in the most gorgeous of trousseaus, bed jackets, mantels, night shawls, boleros, and nightshirts, reflected a sentimental return to the intimate privacy of home life."[1]

"Like slips, nightdresses were soon to embrace the princess line already so much in vogue in the late 1920s. As much decorative fervor could be fostered on a nightdress (with silky materials, fresh colors, and pretty lace trim) as on any evening gown, to the point that, in 1929, nightgowns had become 'veritable, even elegant, little dresses.'"[2] And, "Nightdresses have almost liberated themselves entirely from the notion of being 'undergarments.' They have become independent."[3]

By mid-century, as Farid Chenoune explained in his history of lingerie, "The true guardian of 1950s femininity was the nightgown."[4]

From being a decorous covering for the spouse and occasional symbol of her fragility and vulnerability, the nightgown gradually turned into an erotically charged object that pressed into service all the wiles of fit and length, of see-through fabric and plunging neckline. This evolution culminated in the sensation made by a cropped nightdress worn by Carroll Baker in the 1956 film Baby Doll that gave its name to a brand-new piece of nightwear indicative of a brand-new moral outlook.[5]

IN GENRE FILMS RAMPANT: LIFE IMITATES ART OR VICE VERSA

It is rarely noted that science fiction films were few and far between prior to World War II. In fact, before 1945, science fiction was barely a blip on film. There were Melies's *A Trip to the Moon* (1898), *Just Imagine* (1930), *Things to Come* (1936), *The Invisible Ray* (1936), *Dr. Cyclops* (1940) but not much else. Despite their electric coil labs, even mad scientists like Bela Lugosi in *Murders in the Rue Morgue* (1932), Charles Laughton in *Island of Lost Souls* (1932), Preston Foster in *Doctor X* (1932) and Dr. Frankenstein were perceived for all practical purposes to be dabbling in the *supernatural*.

Spurred by Nazi rocket bombs, the atom bomb and the other *successes* of science, science fiction films supplanted horror movies after World War II. Previously victims of supernatural creatures like vampires, werewolves and mummies, postwar movie maidens fled fungus people, those "moo-tants" or "mu-tates," resurrected dinosaurs, subterranean slime people, flesh-consuming goo, alien invaders, robots, and radioactively-enlarged bugs. The attire of choice for maidens making risky nighttime excursions in pursuit of or pursuit by these creatures: the white negligee.[6]

THE MALA POWERS STORY

An important representative of the white negligee was beautiful Mala Powers, who began her adult film career with two significant 1950 films. In *Outrage*, directed by famous Warner Bros. actress-turned-director Ida Lupino, Mala played the victim in what is generally considered the first mainstream Hollywood film dealing with rape—although Jane Wyman's character had suffered the fate in *Johnny Belinda* (1947). In *Cyrano de Bergerac* (1950), Mala played Roxanne, the title character's cousin, opposite Jose Ferrer's Academy Award-winning turn as the swordsman-cum-poet—and her unrequited lover. Mala traveled to Korea

Mala Powers, *The Unknown Terror* (20th Century-Fox, 1957)

to visit troops—and caught an unnamed disease that laid her up for months, which in Hollywood was often a death sentence.[7] Undeterred, Mala found a niche in "genre" films, i.e., horror and science fiction, B westerns, and dramas.

In these 1950s films, Mala had the opportunity to sport negligees in *The Unknown Terror* (1957), *Man on the Prowl* (1957), and *The Colossus of New York* (1958). The first was a "fungus film" set south of the border where a typical Hollywood mad scientist experimented on the locals in the "Cave of Death." They became night-walking monstrosities. Extraordinarily perceptive on the science fiction cinema, Bill Warren provided his perspicacious opinion on *The Unknown Terror*:

No one should expect all low-budget science fiction movies to be made with intelligence and imagination. Those attributes are in short supply among people in general, and those who make movies are merely people. Sometimes we should be grateful that films are not any worse than they are; occasional glimmerings of intelligence or at least entertainment values should be applauded even if the context in which they appear is inferior. The Unknown Terror is a pretty bad movie in most respects, but it isn't as poor as it might have been; the primary defect is a monster done by a method so foolish that it causes only gales of laughter whenever the picture is shown, which is rarely.[8]

Detergent was the culprit. See photo of a Mala-stalking soap suds man. Note also perfect lipstick and coiffure. Apparently humidity was exceedingly low in this venue south of the border.

In the same year's *Man on the Prowl*, Mala was beset by a more mundane but equally dangerous psychopath in the form of James Best.

Mala Powers, James Best, *Man on the Prowl*
(United Artists/Jana Films, 1957)

The following year's *The Colossus of New York* found Mala disturbed by "dreams" that John Baragrey endeavored to dispel: "And Anne, I promise you. No more lonely hours, no more unearthly sensations, no more voices from the dead. That's all behind us now. Goodnight." But those dreams were real. Mortally injured in an accident, Dr. Jeremy Spensser (Ross Martin) had his brain placed inside a hulking caped robot who visited Mala, asleep in her bed—in negligee.

Mala Powers, *The Colossus of New York* (Paramount, 1958)

NEGLIGEE AS SYMBOL OF OPPRESSION AND LIBERATION

PEGGY WEBBER, THE SCREAMING SKULL (1958)

Peggy Webber has a full resumé as actress in film, on TV, and on radio. She's also directed.

TV's *Mystery Science Theatre* found Webber's movie tailor-made for parody. A five-person cast, a winged-door sports car, a spooky boondocks manse, actor Alex Nicol directing and playing the semi-dimwitted gardener Mickey,

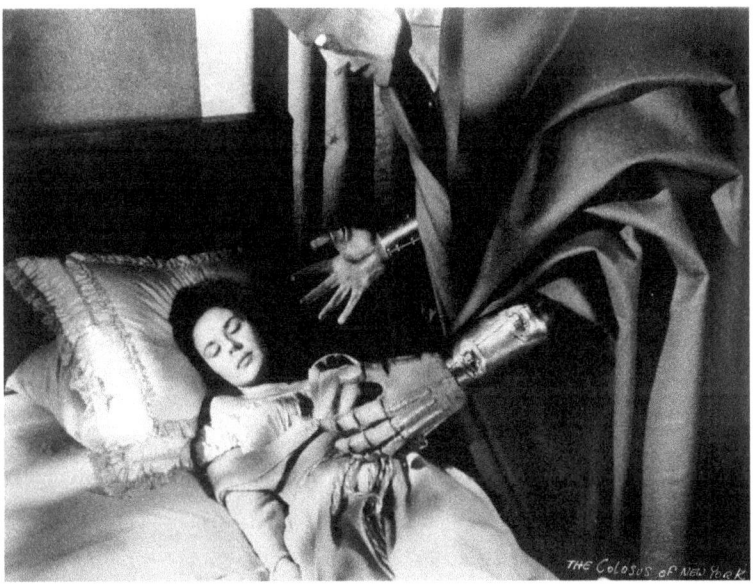

Mala Powers, *The Colossus of New York* (Paramount, 1958)

a heroine (Peggy Webber) inspecting the grounds by night in a de rigeur fifties negligee, and of course a "screaming skull." Well, sort of. But it's all a plot by the husband to drive his wife nuts. This is the movie that begins with a voice telling us that the studio will pay for our burial expenses if the oh-so-shocking ending causes our demise. The common complaint among reviewers, critics, and fans is that *The Screaming Skull* is more likely to bore one to death—a description that could also be applied to its kin, *I Bury the Living* and *Macabre*, both of which were released that same year!

Nevertheless, for aficionados, not much could be better than spending a rainy Saturday afternoon watching this minimalist-cast, minimalist-set potboiler. And there just might be significant subtext. Can something be made of Peggy in a negligee? She's being driven mad by her husband,

Peggy Webber, *The Screaming Skull*
(Madera Productions/American International Pictures, 1958)

driven by night into the dark in negligee, and when she's sitting up in bed it certainly looks as if she's not wearing a bra. And it's a sexy see-through number when she flees the skull, stops, and is silhouetted against the fireplace before collapsing. Oppressed yet liberated?

COLEEN GRAY

Coleen Gray's big screen career is replete with important films. She played opposite Victor Mature in 1947's *Kiss of Death* and was Tyrone Power's co-conspirator in that same year's *Nightmare Alley*. She was Fen, the girl John Wayne regretfully left behind in *Red River* (1948) even after her immortal come-on: "Listen to me, Tom, listen with your head and your heart, too. The sun only shines half the time, Tom, the other half is night." Other significant credits include

Kansas City Confidential (1952) and Stanley Kubrick's *The Killing* (1956). She was a guest star on innumerable TV series.

Besides *The Leech Woman* (1960), one of her genre films was 1957's *The Vampire*, in which she was menaced by John Beal. As for her negligee, "No I did not own the negligee. It was from wardrobe. I returned it. Yes, it was cold wearing it."[9]

John Beal, Coleen Gray, *The Vampire*
(Gramercy Pictures, 1957)

GRETA THYSSEN, AGAIN

Speaking of monsters carrying around beautiful women, let us return to navel-revealing Greta Thyssen—also a stunning specimen in a negligee.

Greta Thyssen, *Terror is a Man*
(Valiant Films/Lynn-Romero Production, 1959)

Greta was at her negligee-wearing best in 1959's *Terror is a Man*, an atmospheric and creepy version of H. G. Wells's *The Island of Dr. Moreau* aptly termed "The original and best Filipino horror film."[10] The trailer told prospective audiences that when the horror became too intense, a warning bell would sound and they could close their eyes until it rang again. The trailer also revealed that Greta's character on that island where Francis Lederer was crafting "a perfect man" was "tormented by unsatisfied desire." Was it any surprise that the "leopard man" fell for and carried her off into the night? It was beauty and the beast again.

Greta guested at Baltimore's Horror and Fantasy Film Society FANEX 9 convention, July 21-23, 1995. She said the Philippine shoot lasted about four sweltering weeks.[11]

BAD GIRLS: THE BLACK NEGLIGEE

On occasion, the dark negligee was favored over the white. How often did that signify that the wearer was, perhaps, loose or evil—the femme fatale? "The historic relationships between sex, death, black fashion, and the female body also help explain the turn-of-the-century emergence of black lingerie's erotic signification."[12]

Anne Francis

Marla English

Greta Thyssen, *The Beast of Budapest* (Barlene Corporation/Allied Artists, 1958)

Anne Helm, *The Interns* (Columbia, 1962)

Carroll Baker, George Peppard, *The Carpetbaggers* (Paramount, 1964)

DID SHE OR DIDN'T SHE ... WEAR A NEGLIGEE?

Movie stars regularly appeared in *Playboy* from early on, but before the mid-sixties, they were not really nude. They wore see-through negligees. Arlene Dahl's nipples were visible through hers in the December 1962 issue. See also "At Home with Kim," the February, 1965 *Playboy* pictorial with Kim

Novak. Besides a gossamer negligee, she shows a bare navel, which she'd exposed for the first time on screen in 1964. (See Chapter 1 for elucidation.)

In so-called real life, American women were wearing negligees. Or, it might have seemed that way. *Playboy* debuted in 1953, and from then into the 1960s, negligees were a routine piece of attire for the Playmates, if not in their centerfold issue, in other photos, such as the Playmate of the Year pictorials or year-end subscription ads. See, for instance, Christa Speck (September 1961, April 1962), Jan Roberts (August 1962), June Cochran (December 1962, May 1963), Toni Ann Thomas (February 1963), Carrie Enwright (July 1963), Jo Collins (December 1964, August 1965), Dolly Read (May 1966), Dianne Chandler (September 1966), Fran Gerard (March 1967). In "real" life, illustrator Alberto Vargas was drawing women in racy attire in the 1940s and later provided many illustrations for *Playboy*.

Where did homemakers, farmers' wives, and small-town secretaries buy lingerie, specifically negligees? Catalogs? Pocket Magazines published such weekly mini-magazines as *Quick* and *Tempo*. These encapsulated worldwide news, quoted celebrities, identified hot Broadway productions, and otherwise gave readers the lowdown on events of the week. The November 10, 1952, issue of *Quick* had a page ad for Frederick's of Hollywood that promoted a quilted housecoat, bikini briefs, a "Sheer Dynamite" Nylon Shorty, and a "Siren" Negligee that was "Inspired by a top Hollywood star! Smoothly molds the figure…wear as gown or robe. Black Crepe-Back Rayon Satin. Sizes 32 to 40…$8.98." In the two-page "Fashion" section of the January 3, 1955, issue of

Tempo a lady modeled "A dreamy negligee. This one of yards and yards of sheer net and Alencon lace. Vanity Fair."

Vanity Fair was joined by Peerless and Top Form in magazine ads throughout the fifties and sixties. Nor were negligees for real women only. They were part of Barbie's ensemble when she was born in 1959.

Anne Randall Stewart (then Anne Randall) *Playboy*'s Playmate of the Month for May 1967, prefers cotton pajamas but wore a negligee in the magazine's 1967 Christmas issue. "The wardrobe belonged to Playboy. If you look through the old magazines, you might even find some other girl wearing it." Anne guesses that women in the '60s did buy negligees from Frederick's of Hollywood. Randall added, "By the way, 'Stacey's' entire wardrobe was purchased there." *Stacey* was the 1973 action-exploitation film in which Anne played a detective. "In Stacey, there was a bedroom scene done in the nude—no negligee."[13]

By the 1970s, centerfold models were more fully uncovered. "Full frontal nudity" was *in*. It became a staple. Negligees were relics of a bygone age of mystery and romance—on the screen and even in girly magazines.

But some non-stars and celebrities must have been wearing negligees. On page L91 of the December 15, 1963, *New York Times*, the Bonwit Teller ad offered "three from a heavenly group of gowns, all full length for purely fabulous sweeps of beauty, all ready to enrapture her on Christmas." On page L98 was the Henri Bendel ad for "Our empire nightgown in crepe de lys (nylon, silk and Dacron)." Note the S.F.A. (Saks Fifth Avenue) ad in the May 2, 1965, issue of *The New York Times*. The drawing of a woman in what might be construed as a negligee has this copy:

NIGHTTIME NYMPHS

Jill St. John, *Who's Been Sleeping in My Bed?*
(Amro-Claude-Mea/Paramount, 1963)
A compromise between negligee and navel revelation.

S.F.A.s Gift-Pretty Boudoir Ensemble with Picot-Edged Ruffling. Black picot-stitching lends a lively staccato note to our opulently ruffled gown and boudoir coat of nylon sheer lined with opaque nylon tricot. Wild rose, blue mist and nude. Petite, small, medium and large sizes. Short gown with self-buttoned shoulder closings, $18; peignoir with rosette-trimmed cuff, $25. Also in long versions, not show: gown, $20; peignoir, $30, small, medium and large.

On that same date, for the impending Mother's Day, Macy's promoted "misty layers of nylon tricot. Send her off to bed in a pampered glow, circled in floaty, feminine dreamwear...airspun, light-as-a-moonbeam surprises by Warner....To top things off, mists of cover in a swishy Peignoir,...." The Lingerie Department was the place.

Curiously, what with our familiarity with the term *negligee*, these ads promoted "nightdresses" and "nightgown." It almost seems as if the term was rarely used and the garment rarely *worn* in everyday life.

On the screen, Jill St. John bridged the gap from negligee to bared midsection in 1963's *Who's Been Sleeping in My Bed?* The film also featured a belly dancer and Jill in a midriff-revealing ensemble.

By the end of the decade, "negligees" remained rare in ads. West Chester, PA's *Daily Local News* of December 4, 1969, featured a large ad for *"Fireside Fashions for her at-home hours. Gift Wrappings She'll Wear all Year..."* There was a nylon quilt shift, pizzazz-endowed culottes, shift gowns, long gowns, mini gowns, pajamas, and long P.J.s. But no "negligee." Closest to that perhaps was, from Katz, "Fuzzy-wuzzy nighty-nights! A dreamy blend of Celanese acetate and nylon. Tricot brushed to a fine fluff in PJ's or granny gown. Dainty flower trim on pink, blue or maize."

CHAPTER 3
HATS OFF!

"I remember once before I didn't have a mere chair for my hat. Dropped to the floor, I had to pick it up myself."
—Sydney Greenstreet, *Flamingo Road*
  (Warner Bros., 1949)

HAT HISTORY

Hats, as we think of them, can be traced to ancient Greece. Hats were practical by keeping heads warm in winter, cool in summer, and protecting the eyes from the sun. They were also expressive.[1] Of paramount importance was designation of the wearer's status. They were a sign of young men coming of age.[2]

But during the twentieth century, hatlessness became common, and has remained so in the twenty-first century, both in Western society and the movies. Rappers and baseball fans might wear visored caps, but in the realm of formal headgear—the bowler, homburg, fedora, derby—their peak passed decades ago.

There are three theories about the cause of our current hatlessness: veterans of World War II rejecting what had been ordered during the conflict, the proliferation of automobiles whose drivers' and passengers' headgear could easily be knocked askew entering or exiting the vehicle, and the perception that President John F. Kennedy did not wear a hat.[3]

At first glance, the Kennedy cause might have some weight. He was a Navy veteran, and, contrary to common wisdom, he did wear hats and had one with him on inauguration day, 1961. The myth is that his perceived hatlessness precipitated a crisis for the hat industry. Yet hat sales, especially dress hat sales, had been in decline since the beginning of the twentieth century.[4]

Not that the hat makers of the United States had taken rejection of their product lying down, as can be witnessed by surveying newspapers where, in the past, each issue provided a plethora of enticing advertisements, such as:

1. The *New York Times* of April 13, 1911, featured a Macy's ad for several men's hats, including the "King Alfonso," which was "a novelty in Men's Hats, a radical departure from the conventional shapes of recent years. It is a faithful reproduction of the hat now being worn by the young Spanish King, whose name it bears." Cost: $2.74.

2. The Wallach Bros. ad in the March 4, 1921, issue of *The*

New York Times: "Beyond question the 'Headease' hat is the most comfortable hat ever devised for mortal man." Or the same issue's Stetson ad: "Every man must judge for himself as to whether he can make his old hat do for Spring—the saving is only a few dollars at most. Hardly worthwhile if one has to feel just a little shabby all the time. Stand squarely in front of the mirror, put on your old hat and look at it. Then drop into the nearest good hatter and try on one of the new Spring Stetson models. You'll get a sense of fresh crispness in your appearance, of Style, of looking and feeling fit. More good, all round satisfaction than penny wise economy could ever give you."

3. The March 15, 1927, *New York Times* ad: "The inimitable Style and Quality that have gained for Dobbs the position of New York's Leading Hatters are clearly perceptible in all Dobbs Hats for the New Season. Three convenient shops. There Is Distinction In Wearing Dobbs Hats." One can but wonder if the chapeau of Fred C. Dobbs, B. Traven's character so ably portrayed by Humphrey Bogart, in a beat up Dobbs-like hat, in *The Treasure of the Sierra Madre* (1948) was inspired by this article.

4. The July 25, 1935, *New York Times* contained the Knox The Hatter ad for the Vagabonds white felt chapeau: "It's a White Hat Summer."

5. The *New York Times* on June 2, 1937: "TUSCAN-AIRE Day" for DOBBS. "Men particular in their dress are choosing the sailor straw hat for hot weather use, and Dobbs sets the style with Tuscan-Aire….impeccably styled but made with a humane regard for the wearer's comfort. Ingenious stitching allows the cooling breeze to circulate freely inside the crown. It's really air-conditioned." Cost:

$5.00. Over at Weber and Heilbroner the Stetson Fantan was the cat's meow in straw. "Here at last is a really new idea in straw hats. Fantan is smartly different, but strictly in good taste. Even the most conservative of men can wear it without a qualm....further cooled by tiny air-vents in the crown."

6. *The New York Times*, December 21, 1949: John David's ad for Mr. Disney hats, including the Otter with hand-felt-edge and suede finish, the "correctly proportioned" Homburg and the Essex. "Amble over to any John David store, tell the salesman you want to get a hat for your Mr. Santa. He'll give you a tiny Mr. Disney hat box with a miniature Mr. Disney hat inside, plus a gift certificate entitling the bearer to the Mr. Disney he wants in the style, size and color he prefers." Mr. Disney Hats went from $8.50 to $40.

7. The *New York Times* ad for Wallachs on April 19, 1955: "The Venture by Lee is an outstanding example of the new featherweight felts you've been hearing about this spring. No longer need you sacrifice style to achieve comfort. The Venture's narrow brim, bound edge and tapered, center crease crown are at the height of fashion—in medium gray as well as the new blackened deep tones of gray and brown. Pre-shaped, of course, to preserve its trim lines permanently." Cost: $10.00.

8. *New York Times*, October 17, 1956: Young's presents "The Stetson Satellite" that was "out of this world." Seeing it would allow you "to appreciate its high style and craftsmanship; touch it, to know extra-mellowness and pliancy in a fur felt; wear it, to see how flattering it can be. Stop in to see it soon. $15." But what was the cause of the "satellite"? There were no man-made satellites in orbit. Sputnik was a year away and that was secret. Were folks being treated to astronomical

discourse in the papers? Maybe some had read Arthur C. Clarke's February 1945 *Wireless World* article predicting communications orbiters. Of course, moviegoers had been inundated with science fiction films since the end of World War II. *Forbidden Planet* came out in 1956. That certainly was "out of this world."

9. The December 30, 1958, *New York Times* ran an ad for the Roger Peet Company and its various hat styles: Brushed Twinley, Homburg, Bowler, Velour Tyrolean, Chesley, and the Semi-velour Telescope.

10. A year later the derby was resuscitated. "After twenty-five years of American obscurity—the style expired with Prohibition and spats—the bowler is back. It made a pebble-sized ripple in men's haberdashery last fall and, by spring, was a Madison Avenue boomlet." Hat Corporation of America was making 3,000 bowlers a week and Adam Hats expected its bowlers to double in sales from 1958. Generally, bowler and derby are similar. Hatters promoted the bowler for all men because it was "dapper," "snappy" and "patrician." "It is the hat for the individual, for the direct thinker and for the young, aggressive Madison Avenue organization man." As for women, who were taking up bowlers/derbies to set off their Bermuda shorts and Chesterfields, I. Benjamin Parrill, the Adam Hats president, found them unsuitable for "the female skull shape. The derby masculinizes a woman. Unless she looks well in English riding clothes or is a double for Greer Garson or Merle Oberon, she should avoid derbies like the plague."[5]

11. Oddities also appeared: On August 18, 1963, the *New York Times* ran a Day Company ad for "Rommel Africa

Corps Sun Helmets With Original Insignia" found in a Belgian warehouse.

12. On December 25, 1968, the *New York Times* featured an Alexander's ad for "MEN'S IMPORTED COATS, SUITS & JACKETS from England, France, Italy & Germany." The six men in the ad are swankily dressed but none sports a hat. 1968 was a key year in hatlessness. Read further.

13. In small-town America, merchants and their ads also changed with the times. In the November 3, 1969, *Daily Local News* of West Chester, PA, thirty miles outside Philadelphia, Bob Norris, "*The STORE Where You 'BELONG'*," equaled big city ballyhoo for a man's wardrobe with multiple paragraph descriptions of suits, blazer, sport coat and overcoat—but no hats. Two men are pictured in modified fedoras but there is no prompt to purchase one. Next day, November 4, the borough's largest department store, Mosteller's, extolled the Grand Opening of the redecorated men's store. You might be "winning a suit, a sport coat, or another valuable piece of clothing...." Perhaps that other valuable item could be a hat but none grace the ad.

14. Move forward to the mid-seventies. *New York Times*, December 7, 1975. It's gift-buying season but hats are hardly, if at all, promoted as a viable present. Coats, sweaters, yes, they are featured. When the man in an ad does has a hat, it's invariably held in his hand at his side, almost invisible.

15. Flash forward to 2011. Panamas to make a comeback.[6]

BUT IN THE MOVIES...

Men's dress hats belonged to that black and white world. They would linger on but be segregated into periods and types. Hats were worn by detectives, by salesmen, by disco dandies, by urban cowboys, by rappers. A young man in a wide-brimmed fedora is passing through his Humphrey Bogart stage; in a narrow-brimmed fedora he is paying homage to Dick van Dyke and the early 1960s; a man in a bowler might be a banker living in his private Edwardian phantasm.[7]

So, for decades, hats were commonplace, ubiquitous, and promoted daily in the papers. And on screen they were much in evidence, ranging from fedoras and homburgs to newsboy caps and, for North African-set films, the fez. Prime examples of the latter include Joseph Calleia in *Algiers* (1938) and Sydney Greenstreet in *Casablanca* (1942). Everyone then knew that Franchot Tone's "You're talking through your fez!" in 1943's *Five Graves to Cairo* meant hat.

Joseph Calleia, Charles Boyer, Sigrid Gurie, *Algiers* (Walter Wanger Productions/United Artists, 1938) Fez meets fedora.

Subtextual meanings were rife. Take 1937's *Lost Horizon*:

Ronald Colman has a wide-brimmed fedora worn at a devil-may-care angle that slants the opposite way from his mustache, so there's no question he's in charge. John Howard, as his kid brother wears his hat more conventionally blocked and angled, so he's second in command at best, and he demotes himself further by being the first to uncover once they're in the getaway plane in which the Europeans ("white people") flee the revolution in China (during WW II the script was changed, and they were trying to escape the murderous Japanese). Edward Everett Horton's bowler identifies him as a comic character. Thomas Mitchell's herringbone cap could go either way, and indeed he does change from a crook on the lam to a valued citizen of Shangri-La.[8]

Humphrey Bogart, James Cagney, *Angels with Dirty Faces*
(Warner Bros., 1938)
"Cagney's fedora almost becomes a character."[9]

Marie Windsor, Charles McGraw, *The Narrow Margin* (RKO, 1952) As with trenchcoats, fedoras were de rigeur for cops *and* criminals.

Most on display was the fedora, headgear of choice for gangsters, gumshoes, police detectives, and journalists ... until the 1970s. Almost simultaneously with the demise of negligees, the man's hat disappeared from the screen except in period films—and sometimes not even then.

Examining *Mulholland Falls* (1996), which is set in the 1950s, some find that it presents "an American past in which the national condition is mirrored by an uncorrupted form of masculinity that will be superseded by the events and transformations of the late 1950s and 1960s. Given the specific outline of the historical epoch that the film invokes, then, the earlier request for, and refusal of, the men to relinquish their head wear assumes far greater significance than simple social decorum."[10]

In the 1930s, the narrow-brimmed felt hat had been seen as proletarian while the fedora signified much more.[11] The "Stetson" was admired and craved. The John B. Stetson hat company made various headgear for both sexes and it wasn't till the 1960s that the Stetson became linked with the cowboy hat.[12]

"By the 1930s the derby's symbolic significance was increasingly used to suggest that the gangster belonged to an earlier era—an anachronism waiting to be expelled from the narrative and the world at large."[13]

In *The Beast of the City* (1932) Walter Huston's chief of police wears a cream homburg. "The height of the hat's crown and its light coloring confirm a sense of the character's decorum and distinction and gives authority to his person in compositions where he is surrounded by his minions, who wear dark fedoras."[14]

No better proof of the pervasiveness of hats on screen in this era can be found than in *Gold Diggers of 1933* (1933). In the final number, "Remember My Forgotten Man," Joan Blondell and Etta Moten sing while, first, men in World War I uniforms march across the stage. Then, as the Great Depression takes hold, these men are still lumbering around but are now out of work, forlorn, forgotten. But they do have hats, most wide-brimmed fedoras or their floppy brim kin. A few have flat caps of the cabbie variety. There might be only one hatless guy amongst the throng.

Symptomatic of a hatted society was the February 13, 1945, issue of West Chester, PA's *Daily Local News*. An almost full-page ad promoted a "Paper Holiday" sponsored by the War Salvage Committee. As "Paper is one of the most critical shortages facing our war effort today," citizens and businesses were urged to go without, i.e., buy merchandise but forego wrapping. "DON'T say, 'Wrap it.' Say, "NEVER MIND WRAPPING IT. It's vital to the war effort." Illustrating the ad are two dozen faces of men and women, all of whom wear hats, for the men mostly fedoras.

Into the 1950s, hats continued their popularity on screen. Take *99 River Street* (1953), with John Payne's ex-boxer, now taxi hack, sporting a flat newsboy or golf cap while the hoods (Brad Dexter, Jack Lambert, Jay Adler) wear the traditional fedora. Until the finale, Dexter never removes his chapeau, and in fact it is taken off only by Evelyn Keyes before he launches her out of his sight. He loses it again in a fight with Payne.

John Payne, Frank Faylen, Gene Reynolds, *99 River Street* (Edward Small Productions, 1953)

But in the fifties, some leading men can hardly be pictured in hats. Picture Tony Curtis, Rock Hudson, and Tab Hunter, the young swains of that era. How difficult is it to remember them in hats in contemporary films? Did studios not want to hide their All-American mugs? Or....

PUNKS DON'T WEAR HATS

Punks and rockers don't wear hats. Of course the Dead End Kids of the 1930s and 1940s were too poor to own them, except for Huntz Hall's ballcap and Leo Gorcey's self-mangled, what, fedora? How about postwar delinquents? Surely some must have had the dough or the moxie to steal their elders' fedoras. But then... hats would equate them with their oh-so-out-of-touch parents, plus the pompadours and various other hairstyles marking them would not be in evidence.

Consider Sidney Poitier (other than in *Duel at Diablo*, can you picture Poitier in a hat?) and Vic Morrow in *Blackboard Jungle*, James Dean in *Rebel Without a Cause*, *The Young Savages*, the Sharks and Jets of *West Side Story*. Even the iconic cap worn by Marlon Brando's motorcycle tough in *The Wild One* (1953) did not start a cinematic trend for teens, even in biker films. (The tendency for bikers not to wear hats began early. A large 1940 photograph on the wall of Jimmy John's Pipin' Hot hotdog stand between West Chester, PA and Wilmington, DE presents five motorcycles, their riders, and girlfriends. None of the guys, whose hair forecasts the style of their 1950s descendants, wear hats. The girls contain their hair with scarves or bandanas.)

STEVE MCQUEEN

Steve McQueen's film career began in the 1950s, and by the mid-1960s this consummate screen rebel had risen into the Hollywood firmament. From his extra and uncredited roles in 1953's *Girl on the Run* and 1956's *Somebody Up There Likes Me*, McQueen was initially an urban tough who forswore the hat. He's a nicer punk in *The Blob* (1958) but again, no hat. On TV's *Wanted, Dead or Alive*, he wears a cowboy hat that's thinner brimmed than most. McQueen's big screen breakthrough occurs as Vin in 1960's *The Magnificent Seven*. But that's a western, going hatless would seem gauche and he uses it as a prop, sometimes said to upstage leading man Yul Brynner. In all of his contemporary-set 1960s movies McQueen eschews headgear. See, for instance, 1962's *Love with the Proper Stranger*, where one would think the New York winter would necessitate a covering of some nature. And McQueen does wear a long coat. But no hat. And no, too, in 1965's *The Cincinnati Kid*, set in the hat-wearing 1930s. Even in 1968's *The Thomas Crown Affair*, where McQueen took a risk playing a financier and wore suits, he did not top it off. Besides westerns and the 1962 World War II films *The War Lover* (pilot's cap) and *Hell is for Heroes* (helmet, but rarely) and 1963's homefront service comedy-drama *Soldier in the Rain*, McQueen *never* wore hats. He even went without in *The Great Escape* (1963). Richard Attenborough and James Garner don military caps but not Steve. He's "Cooler King" Hilts, after all. Cool. That was McQueen's persona and hats did not fit. So it appears that his hatless detective in 1968's *Bullitt* is nothing cinematically significant—for McQueen, but that year is terribly important for Hollywood hats in future. (See "Hat or No Hat" section.)

ELVIS AND HATS

Except when playing a cowboy in *Flaming Star* (1960) and *Charro!* (1969) or piloting a boat in *Girls! Girls! Girls!* (1962)

and a plane in *It Happened at the World's Fair* (1963), Elvis wore no hat. Recalled Anne Helm:

> *The only time I remember Elvis wearing a hat was when he took me for a spin in his new boat. He looked pretty spiffy…it was a birthday present I believe from the Colonel. The boat came with a blue captain's hat which Elvis liked to wear when he was boating. I also remember disguises in the back of the limo when we went out on a date to the movies in Los Angeles. I am sure there were hats among the mustaches as well. Just thinking of Elvis performing in a hat in his jump suits…makes me laugh…a funny image.*[15]

Burt Lancaster, Neil Nephew, John Davis Chandler, Stanley Kristien, *The Young Savages* (Contemporary Productions/United Artists, 1961) Note Lancaster's porkpie lid—a modified fedora and in this instance a symbol of authority.

Harvey Lembeck, *Beach Party* (American International Pictures, 1963) Some punks do wear hats—if they're motorcycle toughs in a comedy under the sway of Harvey Lembeck's Eric Von Zipper.

HAT OR NO HAT

The decade of the 1960s was rushing toward its culmination with a full spate of riveting events. In 1968, came the Tet Offensive in Vietnam, the assassinations of Martin Luther King Jr. and Robert J. Kennedy, and Apollo 8's circuit of the moon. As noted, the MPAA's new film rating system took effect that year. Not perceived at the time was the seminal role 1967-1968 played in the demise of film hats.

Note that police detectives and gumshoes, excepting such as Craig Stevens in *Gunn* (1967) and David Janssen in *Warning Shot* (1967), wore fedoras until the end of the sixties. But, in 1967, Lee Marvin's criminal was hatless in *Point Blank*.

(Contrast with his fedora-wearing bank robber in 1955's *Violent Saturday*.) Frank Sinatra did wear a modified fedora as gumshoe *Tony Rome* (1967) and as *The Detective* (1968). Richard Widmark, Harry Guardino, and James Whitmore wore them in *Madigan* (1968). But 1968 was the turning point. Detective Frank Bullitt (Steve McQueen) wore no hat in *Bullitt*. (He did on occasion don a long coat but, as it was unbelted, it was not the once standard trenchcoat.) Nor did costar Don Gordon, who was adamant: "But I do not and have not worn hats on screen or off."[16]

In 1968's *Coogan's Bluff*, even the police detective in charge, Lee J. Cobb, wears his hat *while sitting behind his desk*. But by film's end, Eastwood has lost his Stetson while pursuing Don Stroud's Ringerman. By 1971, Eastwood is *Dirty Harry* and has... no hat. A sports coat with elbow patches has supplanted it.

Nineteen-sixty-eight was in fact seminal for onscreen hatlessness and is ripe for subtextual investigation. Climate might play a part. Consider the fact that *The Detective* and *Madigan* were set in New York City while *Bullitt* took place in a more moderate clime, San Francisco, thus no hat. And no hat for Marvin in the same environment in *Point Blank*. Yet at the beginning of the decade Glenn Ford's detective wore a fedora while running around the Bay City in *Experiment in Terror* (1962). So there's more than geography and climate at work. A culture of hatlessness had begun, even for civilians. Note 1968's *Charly*. Cliff Robertson won a Best Actor Academy Award for playing a cognitively impaired fellow, but during the time he is "cured"—and hatless—he walks onto a busy Boston street where about 99 percent of the passersby are bare-headed. Note as well that at the very end, when Charly has reverted to his former self and is on a seesaw with the kids in the park he wears a rather crumpled pork pie hat.

Even late sixties TV was affected. *Hawaii 5-O* premiered on September 20, 1968. Did McGarrett (Jack Lord), Danno (James MacArthur) and the rest of their team wear hats? Absolutely not, although there is at least one episode in which Lord, for some reason, does, holding it on near a helicopter's whirling blades.

Clint Eastwood, James Edwards, Lee J. Cobb,
Coogan's Bluff (Universal, 1968)
Three cops in hats but not for long for Eastwood's Stetson.

Anne Helm mused on men's hats and negligees going out of style:

It's one of those questions that makes you think and realize... aha...when did that happen? I miss not seeing hats on men... they all looked so romantic and in charge in a weird sort of way.

I think the planet should all have a hat party! It makes you wonder about other things, too. How about cigarette smoking? You don't see that anymore except maybe in foreign films. I used to be a heavy smoker and when I see one of those foreign films and especially when couples are smoking…it makes me nostalgic for the good old days…How sick is that?[17]

JAMES BOND: "I HAD A HAT WHEN I CAME IN." (THUNDERBALL)

The James Bond series serves as well for a template of sixties movement from hats to hatlessness. 007 was famous for tossing his hat onto Moneypenny's hat rack in *Dr. No* and *From Russia With Love*. In *Goldfinger*, it's Moneypenny who does the tossing after taking the hat from Bond as he's preparing to exit. Bond was not shown entering the office, and he doesn't wear it on his ensuing adventure.

In 1965's *Thunderball*, Connery thinks better of tossing and hangs his hat, but upon leaving it's not there. A Moneypenny souvenir? The film retained the hatted-Bond-figure-and-eye sequence preceding the credits. Ditto for 1967's *You Only Live Twice*, but here the presumably murdered British naval officer is retrieved from the Hong Kong harbor where he'd been consigned to the deep and is unzipped from his body bag, alive and in naval uniform. Entering M's office aboard submarine, Bond tosses his commander's cap onto Moneypenny's hat rack and takes it when he leaves. But afterward there is no headgear.

In 1969's *On Her Majesty's Secret Service*, what many consider the best Bond movie, George Lazenby—substituting for Connery—yanks off a hat in his car at the very beginning when he rushes onto the beach to rescue Diana Rigg, and he does toss it onto the hat rack in Moneypenny's office later. The pre-credits sequence of Bond crossing before our observing eye does feature 007 in a hat. For the most part, however, Lazenby is hatless. In the 1970s, Bond dispensed with headgear, beginning with 1971's *Diamonds Are Forever*, the first of Connery's return as 007. Taking over from Sean Connery, Roger Moore eschewed a hat in his first 007 outing, 1973's *Live and Let Die*, not even wearing one in the pre-credits sequence. When Connery returned again in *Never Say Never Again*, there was no pre-credits eyeball sequence and no hat.

MARLOWE

Extending back in cinematic time but moving alongside Bond and into the future, Raymond Chandler's iconic gumshoe Philip Marlowe was initially, and for most of his film adventures, a hat man. He owned the fedora in the 1940s. See Dick Powell in *Murder, My Sweet* (1944), Humphrey Bogart in *The Big Sleep* (1946), and George Montgomery in *The Brasher Doubloon* (1947). As for 1947's *Lady in the Lake*, star Robert Montgomery had attempted something new: only when Marlowe looked into a mirror was he visible to the audience. Otherwise the *audience* was Philip Marlowe. In those mirror scenes, Montgomery was hatless. Marlowe was absent from the big screen in the 1950s, though other private dicks bore resemblance, such as Ralph Meeker as Mickey Spillane in 1955's *Kiss Me Deadly*. As the sixties ended, Marlowe made a reappearance in a solid film, the eponymous *Marlowe* (1969) with James Garner. But in keeping with the times, Garner wore no hat. Robert Mitchum as Marlowe appeared in *Farewell, My Lovely* (1973) and *The*

Big Sleep (1978). These were period pieces, and so fedoras and trenchcoats were worn. But in *The Long Goodbye*, Elliott Gould went hatless in a contemporary (1973) and rather nihilistic story that left a bad taste in the mouth.

A DISTILLATION OF CHANGE

What significant relationship is to be found between *Take Her, She's Mine* (1963) and *Dear Brigitte* (1964)? Both starred James Stewart. In *Take*, Stewart is aghast at his teenage daughter (Sandra Dee) who has grown up too soon and is wearing an audacious bikini. In *Dear*, Stewart chaperones young son (Billy Mumy) to Europe to meet sexpot Brigitte Bardot. For our purposes here, the significance lies in Stewart's attire. He wears a hat in much of *Take* but does not in *Dear*. Check the posters. Times were changing fast.

CHAPTER 4
SWIMMERS

IMMERSION GENERATIONS

Another cinema tradition, or cliché, which became absent by the 1970s, was the immersion of comely leading ladies into streams, ponds, and lakes. Think of a wagon train stopping at a waterhole, a Virginia Mayo (*The Tall Stranger*, 1957) taking a refreshing dip only to find herself in a compromising situation once clothing-laden bushes are discovered by hero or villain. Even future spacefarers like Leslie Nielsen might stumble upon such a naiad as Anne Francis, paddling about in an arcadian pond on Altair IV in *Forbidden Planet* (1956).

Were these episodes germane to the overall plot or mere titillation?

Freshwater dips have a long history. As previously noted, the lass who accomplishing the extended topless underwater swimming in *Tarzan and His Mate* (1934) was a stand-in, not our favorite Jane, Maureen O'Sullivan.

CONTINENTALS IN THE U.S.

Foreign films were certainly not immune to featuring leading ladies in the buff in the water, even for U.S. release. In *The Indian Fighter* (1955), Italian sexpot Elsa Martinellli played a native American to Kirk Douglas's peace-loving frontiersman. She and Kirk received praise: "Douglas, as the lusty frontier scout, ogles the lovely Indian maiden Onahti—played by Italian actress Elsa Martinelli in her first American film—as she bathes in a pool, and later when they become lovers they are seen frolicking nude in the waters together. It's a refreshing and titillating new insight into old frontier life."[1]

Elsa Martinelli, *The Indian Fighter* (United Artists, 1955)
Contemporary Italian as nineteenth century native American.

Muscle man Steve Reeves was a sensation as *Hercules* (1958). He returned in *Hercules Unchained* (1959), with Sylva Koscina playing Iole and swimming.

Sylva Koscina, *Hercules Unchained* (Galatea Films/Warner Bros., 1959) Modern Italian as ancient Greek.

ANNE HELM

Anne (now Annie) Helm acted in over ninety TV episodes in her career, including roles in *Perry Mason*, *Route 66*, and *Gunsmoke*. Despite possessing genuine (not icky) cuteness and a dynamic figure, she frequently played bad or misled girls. In *Hawaii 5-0* she was both; In 1968's "By the Numbers" she was a mobster's moll, in 1969's "Just Luck, I Guess" an undercover policewoman. Her first feature-length movie was 1960's *Desire in the Dust*. Although she played poor white trash, she snagged wealthy scion Jack Ging. They had a swim scene. Annie says:

> *The swimming scene for Desire in the Dust was probably the most frightening. It was extremely hot when we filmed the movie in Louisiana. All the crew began to joke about the large black water moccasins that reside in the swamp where I was to be submerged with my whole body except my head. It was a very flirtatious scene and the first movie I had ever done. It was so scary for me, I convinced the director in order to play the scene with any validity, they were going to have to find a way to make it safer for me. They built a wooden platform under the water that I could stand on rather than the mud where the snakes lurk…it had wire meshing all around me. Looking back, they just did it to make me believe that the snakes couldn't get to me. But in fact, the snakes could easily swim over the fence that was submerged. From what I understand these snakes are extremely lethal. I recall I wore shorts and a strapless top to give the illusion that maybe I would be naked when you first saw me get out of the water at the end of the scene. How times have changed!*[2]

In 1962, Anne had another exciting swim scene. Playing the Princess Helene, she was secretly observed in a crystal ball by knight errant Gary Lockwood. "It was out on the back lot of Twentieth Century, and I wasn't nude and it was freezing cold."[3] Yet she *seemed* au naturel as she began to emerge. What post-pubescent male didn't exit the theater fantasizing about her? *Mystery Science Theatre* ran the film and when Anne comes up from the pond to her maidservant with towel, Crow T. Robot observes, "precise editing there."

In 2010, Annie recalled, "I don't have a lot of memories about *The Magic Sword* swimming scene except…praying that it would be over soon. It was so very cold that day…It felt like winter and my teeth wouldn't stop chattering. It was filmed on the far back lot of 20th Century Fox, I believe. It was in a very large pond or small lake."4

Anne Helm, *Desire in the Dust*, 20th Century-Fox, 1960
Braving deadly snakes.

JOAN O'BRIEN

Actress and singer Joan O'Brien deserved a longer film career. Recall her screen debut opposite Cary Grant in *Operation Petticoat* (1959). The oh-so-womanly figures of Joan and the likes of Madlyn Rhue made it difficult for the crew to squeeze by them in the tight quarters of the submarine *U.S.S.*

Sea Tiger. Joan almost, but not quite, showed her navel. Her man's shirt was tied at the waist. This was 1959, however....

But, in *Six Black Horses* (1962), another of those small-scale '60s westerns from A. C. Lyles, the standard swim-scene convention was maintained. That same year, Joan reverted to type, playing a nurse in Jerry Lewis's *It's Only Money* and doing it again with Elvis Presley in *It Happened at the World's Fair*.

Joan O'Brien, *Six Black Horses* (Universal International, 1962)

THE BIG STAR IN WATER

Even some really big stars in some really big movies did not eschew immersion.

Although 1960's historical epic *Spartacus* was notable not only for bringing blacklisted screenwriter Dalton Trumbo's name back into the credits and for the somewhat hidden allusions to attempted homosexual seduction by Crassus (Laurence Olivier) of the slave Antoninus (Tony Curtis), the film featured the beautiful and curvaceous Jean Simmons in two risqué scenes as slave girl Varinia. (Is that not a great name?) Early on, Varinia is presented to Spartacus (Kirk Douglas) as his thrill for the night. Her rough tunic is ripped off to reveal a back to rival Kim Novak's. Later, when Varinia and Spartacus are alone in the woods, she takes a dip in a verdant pond. Simmons was initially reluctant to play the scene sans clothes, and so wore panties and bra. But director Stanley Kubrick was disappointed, pointing out that she'd have to stay too low in the water to avoid having her bra visible. Douglas was enlisted to convince her to shuck her duds. On the bank, he made his case. "Jean was laughing. Standing there in the water, she took off her bra and threw it on the shore. She had beautiful breasts."[5]

See also Natalie Wood in *This Property is Condemned* (1966). Yes, her immersion made sense. Down in the deep and hot South she needed some refreshment after recounting to Mary Badham's Willy her dreams of a bright future: "Mardi Gras means carnival. I'm gonna go next year even if I have to ride the rails. And I'm gonna design my own costume out of black, shiny sequins. So that my skin'll look white against it. And I'll glitter when I walk, sparkle when I dance with all those men in masks. And I'll never know who they are, and they'll never know who I am. And I'll dance and dance and dance." Wood's drowning death in 1980 was followed by the revelation that she feared water, making the river scenes in *Splendor in the Grass* and *This Property is Condemned* horribly prescient.

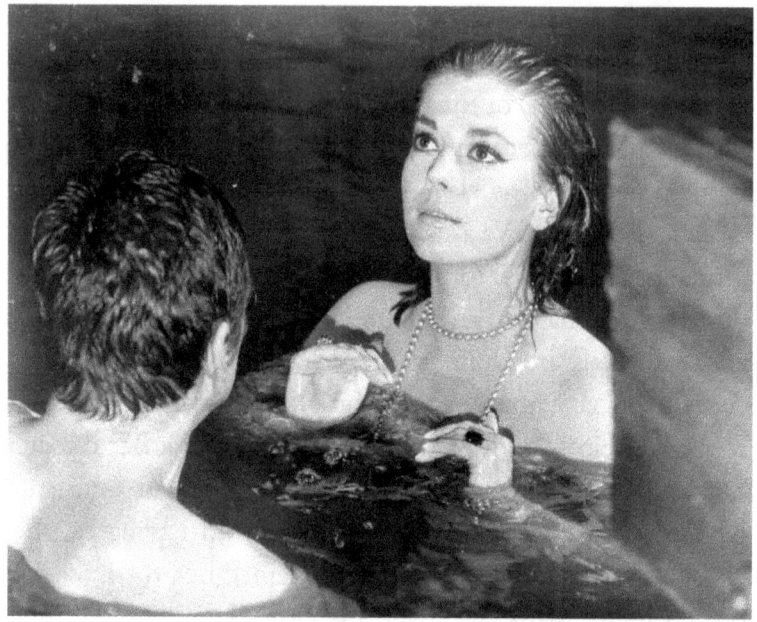

Charles Bronson, Natalie Wood, *This Property is Condemned* (Paramount/Seven Arts, 1966)

SKINNY DIPPING AS METAPHOR

It may be that a 1965 freshwater swim scene sums up the thesis of this book. In the modern-day western *The Rounders*, rodeo-pokes Henry Fonda and Glenn Ford talk hurrah girls Sue Ane Langdon and Hope Holiday into skinny-dipping. Once again, the pond becomes useful for titillation and comedy. Yet there is more here. This swim scene is a metaphor for 1960s cinema, at least as it relates to the movie clichés discussed in this book. At last people have shed navel baubles, negligees, and hats. Everything, in fact. Seeking freedom from societal strictures, they returned to the Garden.

Henry Fonda Hope Holiday, Sue Ane Langdon, Glenn Ford
The Rounders (MGM, 1965)]

EPILOGUE

By now, the reader may have discerned the commonality of the clichés described herein: attire or the lack thereof. It's about divesting oneself of material things: hats, negligees, even bellybutton baubles. Bodies have become free of attire.

Of course, the wearing of negligees did not stop in 1969, but was left mostly to "genre" films, e.g., horror and exploitation, to keep the tradition alive. Britain's Hammer Studios and its Gothic fare continued serving up a plethora of pulchritudinous Brits, Scandinavians, and other Continentals in revealing night dress or no dress at all. To the consternation of some "purists," Hammer added nudity to its horror films.

Kate O'Mara, Kirsten Betts, Pippa Steele, Madeleine Smith, Ingrid Pitt (reclining) *The Vampire Lovers* (Hammer, 1970)

Looking back, one can make a case that the divestiture of the negligee in the course of these films, and presentation of the unadorned female body, was a transition full of meaningful subtext, confirming the informality of modernity.

Hammer Studios' so-called Karnstein Trilogy led the new wave of negligees and nudity. In *The Vampire Lovers* (1970), the Germanic-Slavic Ingrid Pitt, described by one reviewer

Epilogue

Madeleine Collinson, *Twins of Evil*
(Hammer Film Productions/Rank Organisation, 1971)

as "magnificently structured,"[1] essayed Mircalla/Marcilla/Carmilla and savaged many a young maiden. Yes, girl love. This vampiress wore black and white see-through negligees— or nothing at all. *The Vampire Lovers* was a sumptuous feast for the eyes and has been considered "a glistening, erotic production that may well be the most beautiful supernatural thriller ever made."[2]

Twins of Evil (1971) was the sequel and the Collinson

twins, Mary and Madeleine, co-*Playboy* Playmates (October, 1970) took center stage. When Frieda (Madeleine, aka Madelaine) Collinson removed her negligee to seduce an admirer, from the auditorium of the Coleman Barracks Theater outside Mannheim, then West Germany, came a G.I. brother's voice vocalizing the heartfelt sentiments of his kin serving their watch on the Rhine: "Thank ya, Lord, thank ya."

Lust for a Vampire (1971), with Yutte Stensgaard as Mircalla, continued with blood and breasts. And a swim scene allowed Yutte to begin her seduction of Pippa Steele. One presumes that was a still pond because vampires aren't supposed to cross running water.

In the U.S., vampires were back, too, witness *Count Yorga, Vampire* (1970) and its sequel, *The Return of Count Yorga* (1971). But no nudity. Rumor has it that star Robert Quarry nixed it.

Ingrid Pitt had not been loath to disrobe in *The Vampire Lovers*, and she did so as well in *Countess Dracula* (1971).[3] and in *The Wicker Man* (1973).

Swim scenes, like negligees, held on for a time in the 1970s. Lost in the Australian outback, Jenny Agutter found an Eden-like pool for skinny-dipping in *Walkabout* (1971). In the futuristic *Logan's Run* (1976), Agutter and Michael York fled the domed society for freedom of the air—and pond.

As for men's hats, only in "period pieces" would they be worn, and sometimes not even then. One might think that *L. A. Confidential* (1997), which took place in the 1950s, would go hog-wild for fedoras. Not so. Neither Guy Pierce, James Cromwell, Kevin Spacey nor Russell Crowe sport them and are thus in violation of a cinematic and historical convention. Charles McGraw would be flabbergasted.

Seventies blaxploitation films provided an avenue for hats in the characters of pimps, smart dressers, and assorted jive turkeys. But Richard Roundtree's *Shaft* (1971), in keeping with the modern private eye as with detectives, went hatless. So did Thalmus Rasulala in two 1972 releases, *Cool Breeze* and *Blacula*. Secondary characters did not, but the beanie was not exactly designed to promote gravitas.

Thalmus Rasulala, left, *Cool Breeze* (MGM, 1972)
Heist mastermind, no hat; low-level felon, beanie or tam.

Gene Hackman wore a porkpie hat in *The French Connection* (1971) but his partner Roy Scheider did not. Hackman was mostly hatless in *The French Connection II* (1975).

Naked navels continue to this day. Navels and more continued to be bared. See Stella Stevens's groundbreaking love scene with African-American Jim Brown as well as her shower scene in *Slaughter* (1972). Pam Grier goes topless in *Coffy* (1973).

There certainly are other dead movie clichés to examine. Trenchcoats, *women's* hats[4] (check Doris Day in the '60s), bloodless shooting victims, wet bars. And smoking. Recall *Madison Avenue*. Dana Andrews is constantly lighting up.[5]

Devolution, subtraction: negligees to bared bellybuttons to hatlessness to nude swimming. As Warren Hope offered, "It almost sounds like a different world, a world in which women wore negligees and men wore hats. I like this pairing of a change in fashion. I wonder if that's when Americans stopped wanting to be Ladies and Gentlemen and thought it sufficient to be women and men?"[6]

Epilogue

Glenn Ford, *Experiment in Terror* (Columbia, 1962)
Foreseeing the demise of fedoras and navel-challenged women.

APPENDIX A
FRESHWATER SWIM SCENE QUIZ

Match the swimmer and film

1. Omar Sharif
2. Elsa Martinelli
3. Elizabeth Threatt
4. Anne Francis
5. Senta Berger
6. Kim Novak
7. Vanessa Redgrave

8. Joan O'Brien
9. Rosemary Forsyth
10. Joan Taylor

a. *The Tall Stranger* (1957)
b. *The Magic Sword* (1962)
c. *Six Black Horses* (1962)
d. *Cobra Woman* (1944)
e. *Desire in the Dust* (1960)
f. *The Rounders* (1965)
g. *This Property is Condemned* (1966)
h. *The Big Sky* (1952)
i. *Texas Across the River* (1966)
j. *Arabian Nights* (1942)

11. Stella Stevens
12. Anne Helm
13. Sabu
14. Sue Ane Langdon
   Moll Flanders
15. June Allyson
16. Natalie Wood
17. Maria Montez
18. Anne Helm
19. Jean Simmons
20. Fay Wray
21. Terry Moore
22. Joan Crawford
23. Virginia Mayo
24. Julia Adams
25. Maria Schell
26. Jil Jarmyn,
   Carole Mathews

k. *Swamp Women* (1956)
l. *Major Dundee* (1965)
m. *Apache Woman* (1955)
n. *The Amorous Adventures of*
   (1965)
o. *Spartacus* (1960)
p. *Camelot* (1967)
q. *Forbidden Planet* (1956)
r. *The Indian Fighter* (1955)
s. *The Opposite Sex* (1955)
t. *Dancing Lady* (1933)
u. *Cimarron* (1960)
v. *King Kong* (1933)
w. *Mackenna's Gold* (1969)
x. *Advance to the Rear* (1964)
y. *Man on a Tightrope* (1953)
z. *Creature from the Black
   Lagoon* (1954)

Answer Key
1. w., 2. r., 3. h., 4. q., 5. l., 6. n., 7. p., 8. c., 9. i., 10. m., 11. x., 12. b., 13. j., 14. f., 15. s., 16. g., 17. d., 18. e., 19. o., 20. v., 21. y., 22. t., 23. a., 24. z., 25. u., 26. k.

APPENDIX B
GALLERY OF STILLS

"For almost two years, I waded through thousands of never-before-published stills of remarkable quality and unrelenting naïveté. They were so odd, so far removed from anything we see nowadays, that I felt almost as if I'd unearthed the artifacts of some ancient civilization."

Penny Stallings and Howard Mandelbaum, Preface to *Flesh and Fantasy*, 1978

NAVEL ART

Hedy Lamarr, *White Cargo* (MGM, 1942)
("I am Tondelayo.")

Hedy Lamarr, *Samson and Delilah* (Paramount, 1949)
The typical Hollywood exotic but navel-concealing costume.

Barbara Eden
Cheesecake navel allowed, but not on TV's *I Dream of Jeannie*.

Hope Lange, *Love is a Ball* (Gold Medal/Oxford Productions, 1963)
But no bikini in the film itself.

Sue Lyon, *The Night of the Iguana* (MGM, 1964)
No longer Lolita but allowed navel exposure again.

Leslie Caron, *Promise Her Anything*
(Seven Arts Productions, 1965, U.K., 1966, U.S.)

Stella Stevens, circa 1966

Yvonne Craig, circa 1966

Inger Stevens, circa 1966

Michele Carey, *The Sweet Ride* (20th Century-Fox, 1968)

Sylva Koscina, Kirk Douglas, *A Lovely Way to Die* (Universal, 1968)

NEGLIGEES

Robert Mitchum, Jean Simmons, *Angel Face* (RKO, 1952)

Richard Widmark, Marilyn Monroe, *Don't Bother to Knock*
(20th Century-Fox, 1952)
Sexy attire masks dramatic deficiencies.

Elizabeth Taylor promotional still, *The Last Time I Saw Paris* (MGM, 1954)

Gloria Grahame, *The Good Die Young*
(Romulus Films/Independent Film Distributors/United Artists, 1954)

Mitzi Gaynor (circa mid-1950s)

Marla English, *The She Creature*
(American International Pictures/Golden State Productions, 1956)

It Conquered the World (American International Pictures, 1956)

Susan Hayward, Paul Stewart, *Top Secret Affair* (Carrollton, 1957)

Joanna Moore, *Monster on the Campus* (Universal International, 1958) Typical 1950s heroine situation.

Martha Hyer
Material unlimited.

Jeanne Crain, Jeff Chandler, *The Tattered Dress*
(Universal International, 1957)

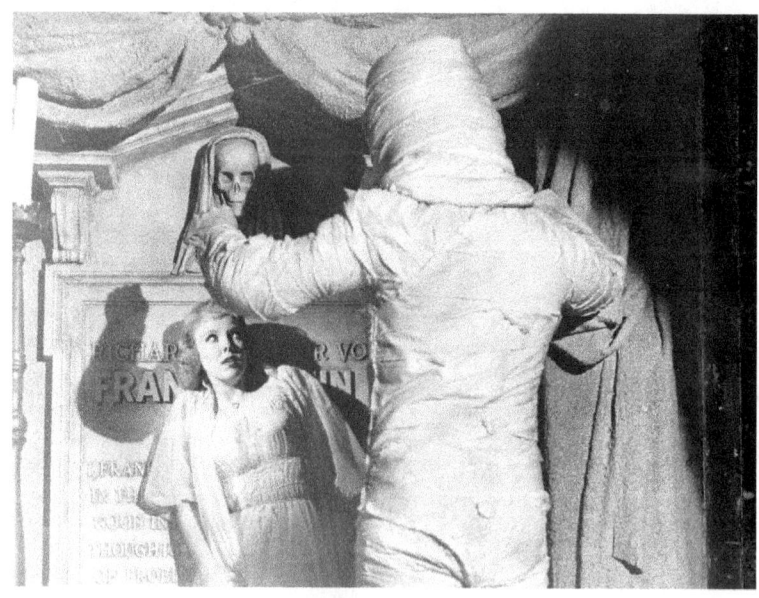

Jana Lund, *Frankenstein—1970*
(Allied Artists/Aubrey Schenck Productions, 1958)

Vincent Price, Myrna Fahey, *House of Usher*
(American International Pictures, 1960)
Nightdress or negligee, you be the judge; it's a period piece.

Claire Bloom, *The Chapman Report*
(Darryl F. Zanuck Productions, 1962)
Racy attire for a then racy film.

Dale Van Sickel, Joan O'Brien, *Six Black Horses* (Universal International, 1962)
Negligee *and* swim scene for Joan.

Gallery of Stills

Ray Milland, Hazel Court, *The Premature Burial*
(American International Pictures, 1962)

Hazel Court, *Masque of the Red Death*
(American International Pictures, 1964)
This caused a stir.

Debra Paget, *The Haunted Palace*
(American International Pictures, 1963)

Joey Heatherton, circa 1964

Joey Heatherton, circa 1964

MEN'S HATS

Victor Mature, Gene Tierney, Phyllis Brooks, *The Shanghai Gesture*
(Arnold Pressburger Productions, 1941)
An exotic movie requires a fez even if set in China.

Joseph Cotten, Hume Cronyn, *Shadow of a Doubt* (Universal, 1943)
Cotten in fedora.

Teresa Wright, Joseph Cotten, Henry Travers, *Shadow of a Doubt* (Universal, 1943) Cotten in Panama.

Dana Andrews, *Boomerang* (20th Century-Fox, 1947) No taboo breakers here.

Victor Mature, *Kiss of Death* (20th Century-Fox, 1947)
The hood goes straight, keeps fedora.

Scott Brady, Roy Roberts, *He Walked by Night*
(Bryan Foy Productions, 1948)
Detectives wear fedoras.

GALLERY OF STILLS

Jane Greer, Robert Mitchum, *The Big Steal* (RKO, 1949)
Mitchum always looked good in a fedora and was
Humphrey Bogart's equal in a trenchcoat.

Lee J. Cobb, Raymond Burr, Anne Bancroft, *Gorilla at Large*
(Panoramic Productions, 1954) Guess who's the detective?

Lee Marvin, *Violent Saturday* (20th Century-Fox, 1955)

GALLERY OF STILLS

Simon Oakland, George Chakiris, *West Side Story* (United Artists, 1961) Lt. Schrank, hatted authority figure; Bernardo, hatless punk.

Frank Sinatra, Jill St. John, *Tony Rome* (MGM, 1966)
Modified fedora, almost porkpie.

SWIMMERS

Julie Adams, *Creature from the Black Lagoon*
(Universal International, 1954)
Adams did the surface swimming.

Vic Morrow, Maria Schell, Russ Tamblyn, Glenn Ford,
Cimarron (MGM, 1960) Typical wagons west waterhole scene.

Gallery of Stills

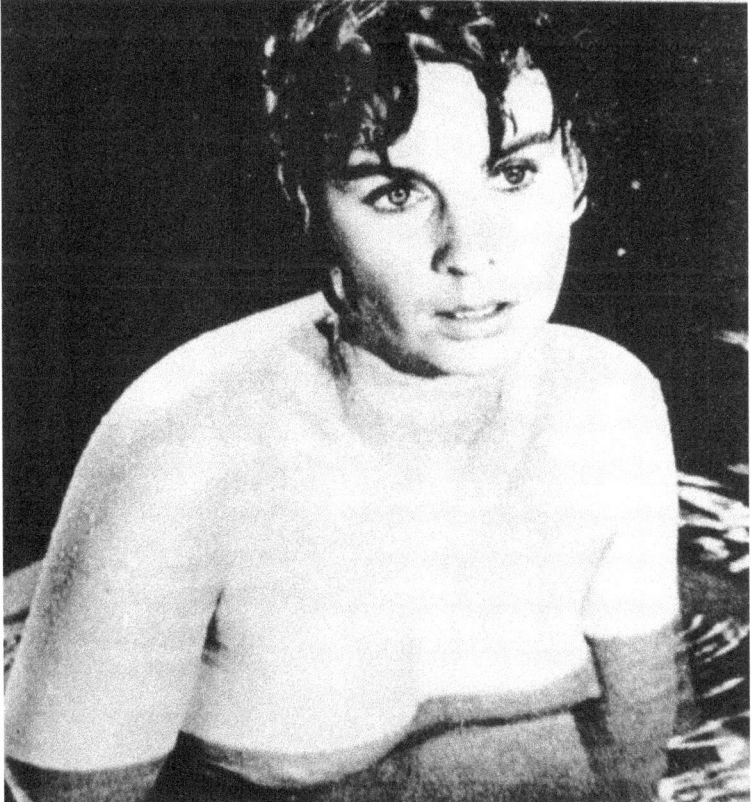

Jean Simmons, Kirk Douglas, *Spartacus* (Universal, 1960)
Jean Simmons may have had the best figure ever.

NOTES

ACKNOWLEDGEMENTS

*"The cultural ground was shifting so fast in the sixties that some filmmakers of that period didn't really know what they were doing, so their work was built on sand." Keith Smith email to author, January 23, 2012.

PROLOGUE

*John Leffler, manager of *Ups-a-Daisy*, a musical comedy at the Shubert Theater in 1928, had invented the hat check system, starting with umbrellas in 1879. "Man Who Invented Hat Check System Still on Broadway," *New York Herald Tribune*, November 4, 1928, p. VII, 4. Or was it perhaps Harry Susskind in 1904? See: Neil Steinberg, *Hatless Jack: The President, the Fedora, and the History of an American Style*. New York: Plume/Penguin, 2004, p. 102.

CHAPTER 1

1. *The Most Dangerous Game, The Palm Beach Story, Union Pacific, Foreign Correspondent, The More the Merrier, Four Faces West, Ride the High Country.*
2. Leonard J. Leff and Jerold L. Simmons, *The Dame in the Kimono: Hollywood, Censorship, and the Production Code from the 1920s to the 1960s.* New York: Anchor/Doubleday, 1990, p. 285.
3. Murray Schumach, *The Face on the Cutting Room Floor: The Story of Movie and Television Censorship.* New York: William Morrow, 1964, p. 168.
4. "Law vs. Anatomy: Chest Goes to Midriff Under Beach Decree," *Philadelphia Inquirer*, February 3, 1944, p. 13.
5. Sally (Forrest) Frank letter to author, January 9, 2012.
6. *Boxoffice*, June 4, 1955, p. 183.
7. Charles Higham, *Howard Hughes: The Secret Life*, New York: St. Martin's Griffin, 1993, 2004, p. 177.
8. Leff and Simmons, pp. 220-21.
9. Joan Collins, *Past Imperfect: An Autobiography.* New York: Simon and Schuster, 1984, pp. 58-59.
10. *Boxoffice Bookin Guide*, June 27, 1955, p. 11 [1794].
11. Novak ranked #9 in the Quigley popularity poll in 1956 on the strength of that success. Marilyn Monroe was #8. It may be surprising to some that neither Rita Hayworth, whom Novak replaced as Columbia's reigning sex symbol, Ava Gardner nor Lana turner ever made the top 10 while Susan Hayward, somewhat out of the public consciousness today, made it three times.
12. Frank Leyendecker, *Boxoffice*, January 4, 1960, p. 18.
13. James K. Loutzenhiser, *Films in Review*, February, 1960, p. 106.

14. Marylin Bender, "Fate of Daring Bikini May Be Decided Today," *New York Times*, July 4, 1960, p. 7.
15. Hanson W. Baldwin, "11 Ships Sunk, 6 Damaged in Maelstrom of Atom Test, *New York Times*, July 26, 1946, p. 3.
16. Patrik Alac, *The Bikini Book: A Cultural History*, New York: Parkstone Press, 2002, p. 21.
17. Patrik Alac, p. 27.
18. Patrik Alac, p. 28.
19. Patrik Alac, *The Bikini Book: A Cultural History*, New York: Parkstone Press, 2002, p. 28.
20. Patrik Alac, p. 29.
21. Patrik Alac, p. 29.
22. Patrik Alac, p. 127.
23. Jill Fields, *An Intimate Affair*, p. 111.
24. Sean French, *Bardot*, London: Pavilion Books Ltd., 1994. p. 10. Larkin's poem is "Annus Mirabilis," 1968.
25. Sean French, p. 16.
26. *Boxoffice*, March 3, 1958, p. 2200-2199.
27. Charles A. Butler, "Brigitte Bardot's Films," *Films in Review*, January 1958, p. 28.
28. Marylin Bender, "Fate of Daring Bikini May Be Decided Today," *New York Times*, July 4, 1960, p. 7.
29. Angela Taylor, "This is the Summer to Take the Bikini Plunge," *New York Times*, May 30, 1966, p. 20.
30. *Boxoffice Bookin Guide*, February 12, 1962, p. 133.
31. Bill Warren, *Keep Watching the Skies: American Science Fiction Movies of the Fifties*, Jefferson, NC: McFarland and Co., Vol. II, p. 542.
32. Murray Wardrop, "Ursula Andress Voted Ultimate 'Bikini Goddess'," *The Telegraph*, August 20, 2009.

33. "California Collections: Amusing Sportwear Designed for the Uninhibited," *New York Times*, November 18, 1959, p. 44.
34. F. Maurice Speed, ed., *Film Review 1958-9*, London: Macdonald & Co. Ltd, 1958, p. 26.
35. Annie Helm email to author, November 16, 2010.
36. After filming the abortive *Something's Got to Give* in which MM had some daring pool scenes, the legend died on August 5, 1962, apparently from an accidental drug overdose. (Conspiracy theorists mull on other causes.) In the film, written by Monroe's recent husband Arthur Miller, Clark Gable drives Monroe to Pyramid Lake, from which she emerges in a full-blown, $300.00 Jean Louis beige bikini. James Goode, *The Story of The Misfits*, Indianapolis and New York: Bobbs-Merrill Company, 1963, p. 181.
37. James Goode, p. 182.
38. James Goode, p. 182.
39. James Goode, pp. 182-184.
40. "Feature Reviews," *Boxoffice*, February 6, 1961, p. 137.
41. Bosley Crowther, *The Misfits*, *New York Times*, February 2, 1961, p. 24.
42. *Time*, February 3, 1961, p. 68.
43. "Nightclubs: The Cooch Terpers," *Time*, January 13, 1961, p. 54.
44. "Nightclubs," p. 57. Hurok was the epitome of the artistic impresario. Among his numerous accomplishments were managing singer Marian Anderson and bringing the Bolshoi Ballet to the U.S. in 1959.

45. Sarah Churchwell, *The Many Lives of Marilyn Monroe*, New York: Metropolitan Books/Henry Hold and Company, 2004, p. 67.
46. Leff and Simmons, p. 230.
47. Dawn B. Sova, *Forbidden Films: Censorship Histories of 125 Feature Films*, New York: Facts on File, Inc., 2001, pp. 181-82.
48. "Hope in a Brand New Package." *Pageant* (January 1963): 38-43, 163.
49. The AIP beach movie chronology:
Beach Party, August 7, 1963 (premiered July 14)
Muscle Beach Party, March 25, 1964.
Bikini Beach, July 22, 1964, (pre-credits features bikini-clad gal showing navel walking on beach; Meredith MacRae and others *and Annette* show navels)
Pajama Party, November 11, 1964. (Susan Hart wilts men and flowers with her dancing and is seen to good effect in the closing credits as she gyrates solo, with Elsa Lanchester and Buster Keaton.)
Beach Blanket Bingo, April 14, 1965. (Trailer shows bikini; bikini during opening credits; Bobbi Shaw wears fur-trimmed bikini and dances with Buster Keaton; *Playboy* Playmate of the Year Donna Michelle barely visible.)
Ski Party, June 30, 1965. (Bikini scene at winter lodge and ends at beach but no close-ups of Yvonne Craig or Deborah Walley.)
How to Stuff a Wild Bikini, July 14, 1965. (Beverly Adams is symmetrical in bikini; Bobbi Shaw is back but in sarong-like item; Buster Keaton as Bwana; Claymation credits; features Playmates Sue (Hamilton) Williams and Jo Collins.)

Dr. Goldfoot and the Bikini Machine, November 6, 1965 (Sue (Hamilton) Williams).

The Ghost in the Invisible Bikini, April 6, 1966. (Susan Hart in most posters has navel airbrushed out.)

50. Annette Funicello, p. 138.
51. Annette Funicello, p. 139.
52. Gail Gerber letter to author, June 5, 2012.
53. Leff and Simmons, p. 251.
54. "Cary Grant and Doris Day Head All-American Favorites," *Boxoffice*, December 14, 1964, p. 9.
55. Joseph Roddy, "Shirley MacLaine: New-Style Star Tries a Rough Role," *Look*, January 29, 1963, p. 61.
56. During fitting on St. Patrick's Day, Novak had some fun by wearing an emerald instead of the rhinestone. See: Larry Kleno, *Kim Novak on Camera*, San Diego and New York: A.S. Barnes & Company, 1980, p. 203.
57. *Boxoffice*, January 4, 1965, p. 71.
58. F. Maurice Speed, ed., *Film Annual 1966-7-8*, South Brunswick and New York: A. S. Barnes and Company, 1967, p. 199.
59. "'Robbery': 'M' for Mystified: Can't Understand MPAA Rating When Other Pix Got Away with Much Worse," *Variety*, June 25, 1969, p. 3.
60. Anne Randall Stewart letter to author, August 19, 2012.
61. Anne Randall Stewart letter to author, August 19, 2012.
62. *Boxoffice*, February 15, 1965, pp. 7-8.
63. Sam Leppard, "Ann-Margret: 'Cinderella Lets Her Hair Down'," *Sound Stage* (June, 1965): 24.
64. Barbara Eden and Wendy Leigh, *Jeannie Out of the Bottle*, New York: Crown Archetype, 2011, p. 159.
65. Eden and Leigh, p. 159.

66. Eden and Leigh, p. 160.
67. "Dogpatch Playmate," *Playboy*, January, 1960, p. 41.
68. Pantyhose was just making its presence known for the masses, soon to be helped by Twiggy and other miniskirt devotees.
69. Rich., *Variety*, December 28, 1966, p. 18.
70. Murray Schumach, *The Face on the Cutting Room Floor: The Story of Movie and Television Censorship*, New York: William Morrow and Company, 1964, p. 280. Further relevant passages from the 1956 Production Code include, under **Particular Applications**, **3. Sex**. 2. (b) Lustful and open-mouth kissing, lustful embraces, suggestive posture and gestures are not to be shown. And under **7. Costumes**. 1. Complete nudity, in fact or in silhouette, is never permitted, nor shall there be any licentious notice by characters in the film of suggested nudity. 2. Indecent or undue exposure is forbidden. See: Murray Schumach, *The Face on the Cutting Room Floor: The Story of Movie and Television Censorship*, New York: William Morrow, pp. 280, 282, 283. Note that navels were not specifically forbidden by the Production Code but presumably fell under "undue exposure is forbidden."

Boxoffice was one industry organ that covered the transformation and previewed the new MPAA code taking effect on November 1, 1968.

Despite its long opposition to statutory film classification, which was deemed to be a form of censorship, the industry had to recognize the necessity of meeting the demands of the changing times and conditions surrounding the exhibition of motion pictures. The move it has made will serve to keep control of its products in its own hands, as it were, and make possible the rendering of a greater service to the public; to keep it properly informed on the content of its films and their suitability for the varying types of audiences, to all of whom the industry must cater. See: Ben Shlyen, "For Freedom of the Screen," *Boxoffice*, October 14, 1968, p. 2.

The new system received endorsements by religious organizations, such newspapers as the *New York Times*, and other communications media. But the road was deemed hard and to be trod carefully lest there be significant setbacks. "In other words, strict adherence to the program is essential to its success." See: Ben Shlyen, p. 2.

The change was examined in some depth. A press conference was held in New York where Jack Valenti, president of the Motion Picture Association of America, general counsel Louis Nizer, National Association of Theatre Owners president Julian S. Rifkin, and Munio Podhorzer of the International Film Importers & Distributors of America were present. The categories for films were examined: G for General, M (Suggested for Mature Audiences), R, or Restricted, where those under 16 would not be admitted unless accompanied by a parent or guardian, and X, where those under 16 were not to be admitted. There were two categories under X: those films submitted to the Code and Rating Administration which received an X due to the treatment of sex, violence, crime or profanity, and those films *not* submitted for inspection.

Valenti said that censorship and classification by law are wrong, are intrusions into a communications art form shielded and protected by the First Amendment, adding that the screen should be free for filmmakers just as it is for writers, publishers, and others. "But," the MPAA head said, "we must never make motion pictures for just one audience. There are many audiences and if we seek out the lowest common denominators, we will find ourselves making movies that would be, as one Supreme Court justice put it, inane." Although the industry should not base boundaries on children, "we can be concerned about children. The creative filmmaker ought to be free to make movies for a variety of tastes and audiences, with a sensitive concern for children. See: "Voluntary Rating System on Films Will Start Nov. 1," *Boxoffice*, October 14, 1968, p. 3.

Communicating the plan to the public was deemed essential. See "Voluntary Rating System," p. 4.

In tandem with the Production Code, the newly christened Code and Rating Administration was to administer the new system of ratings. See "Voluntary Rating System," p. 4.

Valenti went on the road to describe and discuss the new plan. One stop was Buck Hill Falls, in Pennsylvania's Pocono Mountains, where he addressed the annual convention of Pennsylvania elementary school principals. Valenti said the plan belonged to the public, who would determine its success or failure. Youth, "outside of school, today's youth is immersed on the film medium." Thus, "We need to enhance the ability of children and young adults to learn and understand and discriminate through viewing and listening, as well as reading." See: "Success of Film Rating Plan Rests with American Public, Says Valenti,"

Boxoffice, November 11, 1968, p. 9.
71. "ACE Moves to Urge MPA to Strengthen Film Code," *Motion Picture Herald*, April 22, 1961, p. 7.
72. "Rating System OKd By U.S. Film Industry," *Philadelphia Inquirer*, October 8, 1968, p. 30.
73. "Catholic Ratings Expect to Go On," *Variety*, October 16, 1968, p. 5.
74. A list of the first 72 feature films rated under the new system appeared in *Boxoffice*. See: "Motion Pictures Rated by the Code and Rating Administration, *Boxoffice*, November 18, 1968, p. 11. Two received the X rating: *Birds in Peru*, the French-made, Jean Seberg starrer in which she played a nymphomaniac, and *The Girl on a Motorcycle* with Marianne Faithful chasing her lover. R ratings went to *Corruption* (horror violence), *Dead Run* (violence), *The Fox* (lesbianism), *The Hooked Generation* (drugs), *Joanna* (swinging London, pregnancy), *Lady in Cement* (1968), *The Magus* (1968), *The Night of the Following Day* (1968; violence, nudity), *On My Way to the Crusades, I Met a Girl Who...* (1967; Italy, spoof), *Payment in Blood* (aka *Renegade Riders*, 1967; Italy, violence), *The Princess* (aka *A Time in the Sun*; 1966; Sweden), [*The*] *Riot* (1969; violence), *The Sergeant* (homosexuality), *The Shame* (aka *Shame*; 1968; violence/war; Sweden), *Three in the Attic* (1968; sex), *The Touchables* (1968; U.K.; sex), and *2000 Years Later* (1969, spoof). Note that most of the preceding were not U.S. films. Europe was still ahead in *adult* content.

This freedom of expression via navels and nudity did not last. Feminist objections to objectification of women, Congressional witch hunts of the media—these were

some reasons. Hypocritically, violence was almost given a free pass in feature films if not on TV.
75. "MPAA Ratings to Now: G(43), M(29), R(22); Puzzle: X for 'Birds' But R for 'The Fox'," *Variety*, December 4, 1968, p. 18.
76. "Exhibitor Support is Key to Rating Plan Success," *Boxoffice*, November 18, 1968, p. 5.]
77. It received the M or Mature rating from the MPAA "evidently, to the extensive burlesque footage, especially Miss Ekland's, including a very, very fast shot of bare breasts when her costume falls apart...." Robe., *Variety*, December 4, 1968, p. 6.
78. Roi Frumkes, *Films in Review*, April 1968, p. 242.

CHAPTER 2

1. Farid Chenoune, *Hidden Underneath: A History of Lingerie*. New York: Assouline Publishing, 2005, p. 80.
2. Chenoune, p. 80; inside quote from *Mon Trousseau, Linge de corpse et de maison. Manual general 1928-1929*, p. 9.
3. *La Belle Lingerie*, summer 1935, in Chenoune, p. 80.
4. Chenoune, p. 110.
5. Chenoune, *Hidden Underneath*, p. 110.
6. Sprinkled among the non-genre films were mainstream offerings: Eleanor Parker, *The Naked Jungle* (1953), Grace Kelly, *Dial M for Murder* (1954).
7. Kim Holston, "FANEX 12: End of an Era?", *Film Ex*, Spring 1999, p. 12. Yvonne Craig, veteran of a score of feature films and TV's Batgirl, also spoke of slackening off in Hollywood. "and it's well known that when you are cool, you are COLD." Kim Holston, *Starlet: 54 Famous*

and Not So Famous Leading Ladies of the Sixties, Jefferson, NC: McFarland & Company, p. 45.
8. Bill Warren, *Keep Watching the Skies: American Science Fiction Movies of the Fifties, Volume I: 1950-1957*, Jefferson, NC: McFarland & Co., 1982 , p. 397.
9. Coleen Gray letter to author, April 6, 2012.
10. Michael Weldon, *The Psychotronic Encyclopedia of Film*, New York: Ballantine Books, 1983, p. 700.
11. "FANEX 9," *Film Ex*, Summer 1995, p. 8.
12. Jill Fields, *An Intimate Affair: Women, Lingerie, and Sexuality*, Berkeley: University of California Press, 2007, p. 114.
13. Anne Randall Stewart letter to author, August 19, 2012.

CHAPTER 3

1. Neil Steinberg, *Hatless Jack: The President, the Fedora, and the History of an American Style*. New York: Plume/Penguin, 2004, p. xv. Of paramount importance was designation of the wearer's status. They were a sign of young men coming of age.
2. Steinberg, p. xvi.
3. Neil Steinberg, *Hatless Jack*, p. xix.
4. Neil Steinberg, *Hatlass Jack*, p. xix. Another probable myth is that Clark Gable caused a crisis in the men's underwear industry when he went t-shirt-less in 1934's *It Happened One Night*. Legend has it T-shirt sales plummeted. What of the opposite side of the coin, that what movie characters wore spurred sales? Did short denim and leather jackets worn by Marlon Brando in *The Wild One* (1953) and James Dean in *Rebel Without a Cause* (1955) create a huge demand? Was it possible that, as Kathy

Spicciati said, Lee Marvin invented the V-neck t-shirt in *Shack Out on 101* (1955). [Kathy Spicciati to author] And did Brando *wearing* a t-shirt in 1951's *A Streetcar Named Desire* cause sales to escalate?
5. Marylin Bender, "Derby Back for Men, Too," *New York Times*, August 6, 1959, p. 30.
6. Panamas were scheduled for a comeback in 2011. David Morgan ran an ad in the June 2011 issue of *The Atlantic* promoting the Panama Fedora and the Darwin Panama. The first was "hand woven in Ecuador from toquilla fiber. Grosgrain ribbon band, water resistant coating." $75.00. The Darwin went for $95.00 and was also of toquilla fi ber with Australian styling. It was water resistant and had a braided kangaroo leather band.

In 2012 Bradford Dillman wrote, "One time I was a late arrival to the cast of a Movie of the Week, so late I was asked to carry my wardrobe aboard the flight to Nassau.

The wardrobe consisted of a flamboyant silk shirt, tight trousers, and a broad-brimmed Panama hat. I'd already decided it would be a colorful acting choice to play the character as gay. I [had] no sooner shaken hands with the director than he said, 'This pilot is to star the young man working with you in this scene." He called, 'Oh, Lance? Come meet Bradford Dillman.'

Lance came in flying higher than a 747. Squeezing my hand, he shrilled, 'Well Hi! I can't tell you! What a treat! I'm such a fan!' Decision time. Do I junk the notion or do I forge boldly ahead? I forged.

As I expected Lance had done his own homework. He set his jaw, squared his shoulders and dropped his voice three octaves to bury the sibilance. It made a nice counterpoint to my bird's-wing fluttering.

Terribly confused, the star avoided off-camera communication with me for the duration." Bradford Dillman letter to author, October 7, 2012.
7. Steinberg, p. 294.
8. Keith Smith email to author, July 11, 2012.
9. "Cagney's fedora almost becomes a character." Keith Smith, "DVD Briefs: *Angels with Dirty Faces*," *Film Ex*, Winter 2008, p. 6.
10. Esther Sonnet and Peter Stanfield, "Good Evening Gentlemen; Can I Check Your Hats Please? Masculinity, Dress and the Retro Gangster Cycles of the 1990s," in Grieveson, Lee; Sonnet, Esther; and Stanfield, Peter, eds., *Mob Culture: Hidden Histories of the American Gangster Film*, New Brunswick, NJ: Rutgers University Press, 2005, p 165.
11. *Mob Culture*, p. 167.
12. *Mob Culture*, p. 168.
13. *Mob Culture*, p. 171.
14. *Mob Culture*, p. 172.
15. Annie Helm email to author, August 9, 2012.
16. Don Gordon letter to author, November 26, 2012.
17. Annie Helm email to author, November 17, 2010.

CHAPTER 4

1. Tony Thomas, *The Films of Kirk Douglas*, Secaucus, NJ: Citadel Press, 1972, p. 128.
2. Annie Helm email to author, November 16, 2010.
3. "Anne Helm Interviewed by Kim Holston," *Film Ex* (Winter, 2000), p. 2.

4. Echoing Annie Helm's sentiments about the 20th Century-Fox backlot pool, Coleen Gray recalled a *Las Vegas Shakedown* swim scene. This was not a rustic pool, but a hotel one. "I remember one on location in Las Vegas—January. Cold—the crew wore heavy jackets. It was torture having to get into the water and then shiver in the cold air when coming out. I think they cut that scene." Coleen Gray letter to author, April 6, 2012.
5. Kirk Douglas, *I Am Spartacus! Making a Film, Breaking the Blacklist*, New York: Open Road, 2012, pp. 109-110.

EPILOGUE

1. Alan Dodd, *L'Incroyable Cinema*, Spring 1971, p. 35.
2. Kurt Brokaw, *A Night in Transylvania: The Dracula Scrapbook*, New York: Grosset & Dunlap, 1976, p. 110.
3. A Holocaust survivor. Ingrid Pitt had escaped their replacement totalitarians—the Communists—in East Germany, fled to England and started making movies, soon to be almost exclusively those of the fantastic genres. Her international break came when she played Heidi the barmaid in the Richard Burton-Clint Eastwood World War II extravaganza *Where Eagles Dare* (1969). As Burton's character said, "She's been one of our top agents in Bavaria since 1941, and, ah, what a disguise." Pitt related a navel tale in 1984:

One funny thing that happened was in Countess Dracula, when Sandor Eles lost his moustache. There we were sensually sexying away in the haystack when he lovingly looks up at me after nuzzling in my cleavage and lo & behold: half his moustache is missing! I corpse to the consternation of Peter

Sasdy who couldn't see his face since the shot was over Sandor's shoulder. We searched everywhere for that bloody moustache, the make-up man, the haystack, my wig, my ears, my bosom: nothing!

That evening I lie in my bath and there's the moustache peeking out of my navel. Now I ask you: how in hell did that thing work its way through the corset, through the tight belts and five skirts to my navel? Am I, I ask myself, the only woman with a moustache in her navel? [Ingrid Pitt letter to author, 1984]

4. Jane Maas has an amusing description of sixties professional women wearing hats during work in *Mad Women: The Other Side of Life on Madison Avenue in the '60s and Beyond*, New York: Thomas Dunne Books, 2012, pp. 114-115.

5. To track the history of onscreen smoking, examine *The Devil is a Woman* (1935), where Marlene Dietrich works in a cigarette factory, Robert Mitchum in *Out of the Past* (1947), and *The Quiet Man* (1952), in which John Wayne flicks away innumerable butts.

6. Warren Hope, Ph.D, email to author, October 29, 2010.

REFERENCES

ARTICLES

"ACE Moves to Urge MPA to Strengthen Film Code." *Motion Picture Herald*, April 22, 1961, p. 7.

"Anne Helm Interviewed by Kim Holston," *Film Ex* (Winter, 2000), p. 2.

Baldwin, Hanson W. "11 Ships Sunk, 6 Damaged in Maelstrom of Atom Test." *New York Times*, July 26, 1946, pp. 1, 3.

Bender, Marylin. "Derby Back for Men, Too." *New York Times*, August 6, 1959, p. 30.

Bender, Marylin. "Fate of Daring Bikini May Be Decided Today." *New York Times*, July 4, 1960, p. 7.

"FANEX 9." *Film Ex* (Summer 1995): 8. [re Greta Thyssen]

Holston, Kim. "Anne Helm Interviewed by Kim Holston." *Film Ex* (Winter, 2000): 1-5.

Holston, Kim. "FANEX 12: End of an Era?" *Film Ex* (Spring, 1999): 11-12. [re Mala Powers]

"Hope in a New Package." *Pageant* (January 1963): 38-43.

"Law vs. Anatomy: Chest Goes to Midriff Under Beach Decree," *Philadelphia Inquirer*, February 3, 1944, p. 13.

Leppard, Stan. "Ann-Margret: 'Cinderella Lets Her Hair Down'," *Sound Stage* (June, 1965): 18-27, 88.

Little Shoppe of Horrors (August, 2004). Includes "The Making of *The Vampire Lovers*" by Bruce G. Hallenbeck, "The Making of *Lust for a Vampire*" by Elandra Kirsten Meredith and Oscar Martinez, and "The Making of *Twins of Evil*" by Bruce G. Hallenbeck.

"Motion Pictures Rated by the Code and Rating Administration," *Boxoffice*, November 18, 1968, p. 11.

"Nightclubs: The Cooch Terpers." *Time*, January 13, 1961, pp. 54, 57.

"Peggy Webber." Interviewed by Kim Holston. *Film Ex* (Spring 2009): 6-7.

"Problems in Rating Plan; Exhibitor is Key Man," *Boxoffice*, November 4, 1968, p. 5.

"Rating System OKd By U.S. Film Industry," *Philadelphia Inquirer*, October 8, 1968, p. 30.

"'Robbery': 'M' for Mystified: Can't Understand MPAA Rating When Other Pix Got Away with Much Worse." *Variety*, June 25, 1969, p. 3.

Roddy, Joseph. "Shirley MacLaine: New-Style Star Tries a Rough Role." *Look*, January 29, 1963, pp. 60-65.

Shlyen, Ben. "For Freedom of the Screen," *Boxoffice*, October 14, 1968, p. 2.

Smith, Keith. "DVD Briefs: *Angels with Dirty Faces.*" *Film Ex* (Winter 2008): 6.

"Success of Film Rating Plan Rests with American Public, Says Valenti," *Boxoffice*, November 11, 1968, p. 9.

Taylor, Angela. "This is the Summer to Take the Bikini Plunge." *New York Times*, May 30, 1966, p. 20.

"Voluntary Rating System on Films Will Start Nov. 1," *Boxoffice*, October 14, 1968, pp. 3-4.

BOOKS

Alac, Patrik. *The Bikini: A Cultural History.* Translated from the French by Mike Darton. New York: Parkstone Press, 2002.

Bensimon, Kelly Killoren. *The Bikini Book.* New York: Thames & Hudson, 2006.

Chenoune, Farid. *Hidden Underneath: A History of Lingerie.* New York: Assouline Publishing, 2005.

Collins, Joan. *Past Imperfect: An Autobiography.* New York: Simon and Schuster, 1984.

Fields, Jill. *An Intimate Affair: Women, Lingerie, and Sexuality.* Berkeley: University of California Press, 2007.

French, Sean. *Bardot.* London: Pavilion Books Ltd., 1994.

Funicello, Annette, and Romanowski, Patricia. *A Dream is a Wish Your Heart Makes: My Story.* New York: Hyperion, 1994.

Gardner, Gerald. *The Censorship Papers: Movie Censorship Letters from the Hays Office, 1934 to 1968.* New York: Dodd, Mead & Company, 1987.

Goode, James. *The Story of The Misfits.* Indianapolis and New York: Bobbs-Merrill Company, 1963.

Grieveson, Lee; Sonnet, Esther; and Stanfield, Peter, eds. *Mob*

Culture: Hidden Histories of the American Gangster Film. New Brunswick, N: Rutgers University Press, 2005. See, in particular: Esther Sonnet and Peter Stanfield, "Good Evening Gentlemen; Can I Check Your Hats Please? Masculinity, Dress, and the Retro Gangster Cycles of the 1990s," pp. 163-184.

Heard, Marcus. *Hammer Glamour: Classic Images from the Archive of Hammer Films*. London: Titan Books, 2009.

Higham, Charles. *Howard Hughes: The Secret Life*. New York: St. Martin's Griffin, 1993. Prologue, 2004.

Holston, Kim. *Starlet: Biographies, Filmographies, TV Credits and Photos of 54 Famous and Not So Famous Leading Ladies of the Sixties*. Jefferson, NC: McFarland & Co., 1988.

Kleno, Larry. *Kim Novak on Camera*, San Diego and New York: A.S. Barnes & Company, 1980.

Leff, Leonard J., and Simmons, Jerold L. *The Dame in the Kimono: Hollywood, Censorship, and the Production Code from the 1920s to the 1960s*. New York: Anchor/Doubleday, 1990.

Playboy. *Playboy's Vargas Girls*. Chicago: Playboy Press, 1972.

Ponzi, Maurizio. *The Films of Gina Lollobrigida*. Secaucus, NJ: Citadel Press, 1982.

Schumach, Murray. *The Face on the Cutting Room Floor: The Story of Movie and Television Censorship*. New York: William Morrow, 1964.

Sova, Dawn B. *Forbidden Films: Censorship Histories of 125 Motion Pictures*. Foreword by Marjorie Heins. New York: Facts on File, Inc., 2001.

Speed, F. Maurice, ed., *Film Review 1958-9*. London: Macdonald & Co. Ltd, 1958.

Speed, F. Maurice, ed. *Film Review 1962-1963*. London: Macdonald & Co., 1962.
Stallings, Penny, with Mandelbaum, Howard. *Flesh and Fantasy*. New York: St. Martin's Press, 1978.
Steinberg, Neil. *Hatless Jack: The President, the Fedora, and the History of an American Style*. New York: Plume/Penguin, 2004.
Strick, Marv, and Lethe, Robert I. *The Sexy Cinema*. Los Angeles: Sherbourne Press, 1975.
Sullivan, Steve. *Va Va Voom!* Los Angeles: General Publishing Group (Rhino), 1995.
Sullivan, Steve. *Glamour Girls: The Illustrated Encyclopedia*. New York: St. Martin's Griffin, 1999.
Thomas, Tony. *The Films of Kirk Douglas*. Secaucus, NJ: Citadel Press, 1972.
Warren, Bill. *Keep Watching the Skies! American Science Fiction Movies of the Fifties, Volume II: 1958-1962*. Jefferson, NC: McFarland & Co., 1986.

FILM ADVERTISEMENTS
Bird of Paradise, Boxoffice, September 8, 1932, pp. 6-7.
Son of Sinbad, Boxoffice, May 7, 1955, p. 23.

FILM REVIEWS
And God Created Woman, Boxoffice, March 3, 1958, p. 2200-2199.
Land of the Pharaohs, Boxoffice Bookin Guide, June 27, 1955, p. 11 [1794].
The Misfits, Time, February 3, 1961, p. 68.
Son of Sinbad, Boxoffice, June 4, 1955, p. 183.
Solomon and Sheba, Boxoffice, January 4, 1960, p. 18.

Voyage to the 7th Planet, *Boxoffice Bookin Guide*, February 12, 1962, p. 133.

LETTERS AND EMAILS
Ingrid Pitt letter to author, 1984.
Annie Helm email to author, November 16, 2010.
Sally Forrest letter to author, January 9, 2012.
Coleen Gray letter to author, April 6, 2012.
Gail Gerber letter to author, June 5, 2012.
Annie Helm email to author, August 9, 2012.
Anne Randall Stewart letter to author, August 19, 2012.

ALSO FROM BEARMANOR MEDIA

bearmanormedia.com

www.ingramcontent.com/pod-product-compliance
Lightning Source LLC
Chambersburg PA
CBHW051922160426
43198CB00012B/1997